What happens when a respected pastor in a historic evangelical denomination suddenly discovers the supernatural power of the Holy Spirit? He has no choice— he must testify about the remarkable conversions, the physical healings and the other Book of Acts manifestations that inevitably follow. Charles Carrin's astonishing story is must reading for every believer who is willing to experience the miracle-working power of the Holy Spirit in his or her own life!

—ROBERT WALKER
FOUNDING EDITOR OF *CHRISTIAN LIFE* MAGAZINE
AND FORMER ASSISTANT PROFESSOR OF JOURNALISM
AT WHEATON COLLEGE

The Edge of Glory is for anyone who wants all that God has to give! We've never read a book that kept us captivated like this one; we simply could not put it down. Charles Carrin's words are power-packed and life-changing, from the first to the last. If you are hungry for God's miracle-working power in your life, this is a must-read!

—CHARLES AND FRANCES HUNTER
THE HAPPY HUNTERS
HUNTER MINISTRIES

THE EDGE OF GLORY

*Receiving the Power
of the Holy Spirit*

Charles Carrin

CREATION
HOUSE
PRESS

THE EDGE OF GLORY
RECEIVING THE POWER OF THE HOLY SPIRIT
by Charles Carrin
Published by Creation House Press
A part of Strang Communications Company
600 Rinehart Road
Lake Mary, Florida 32746
www.creationhouse.com

Unless otherwise noted, all Scripture quotations are taken
from the New King James Version of the Bible.
Copyright © 1979, 1980, 1982 by Thomas Nelson, Inc.,
publishers. Used by permission.
Scripture quotations marked KJV are from the King James
Version of the Bible. Scripture quotations marked NLT are from
the Holy Bible, New Living Translation, copyright © 1996.
Used by permission of Tyndale House Publishers, Inc.,
Wheaton, IL 60189. All rights reserved.

Library of Congress Catalog Card Number: 2001086710
International Standard Book Number: 0-88419-776-X

01 02 03 04 05 – 7 6 5 4 3 2 1

Printed in the United States of America

Dedication

Dedicated to those faithful servants
in every Christian fellowship
who are determined
to go all the way
with God.

✝

Acknowledgments

My heartfelt gratitude goes to
Harvey and Vera Patrick,
Carolyn Folena,
My family,
The members of my Board, and
The diligent work of my secretary,
Karen McMichael
Thank you!
CCC

Contents

Foreword by Jack Taylor vii

Foreword by R.T. Kendall......................ix

Preface xii

Introduction xiii

1 How It All Began..............................1

2 Anointing: The Fragrance of Jesus 15

3 The Holy Spirit's Charisma Gifts Are
Available to You..................................35

4 You Can Minister in the Power of
the Holy Spirit..................................53

5 Jesus Has an "Engagement Ring" for You 71

6 History That Encourages: God Used
Others Like You..................................83

7 Beware the Demon of Unbelief 115

8 God's Five-Fold Ministry and Satan's
Five-Fold Opposition 127

9 Apostasy and Occultism Will Oppose You ..147

10 Spiritual Warfare: You Have Authority
Over Demons 159

11 Finale: Release of Power From Your
Inner Person 175

Appendix A:
The Ministry of the Holy Spirit...................185

Appendix B:
The Believer's Authority Over Demons........191

Foreword

I was drawn to the ministry of Charles Carrin first through his book *Sunrise of David/Sunset of Saul.* A friend had encountered Charles and was greatly blessed by his ministry. I read the book and was smitten at the combination of brevity, relevance and no-holds-barred, to-the-point communication. I then met Charles as we shared the platform in a conference  years later. His message and ministry were consistent with his writing. It was hard-hitting, direct, confrontational, anointed.

Since that time we have shared meaningful hours together in fellowship, and I am delighted to commend this new work *The Edge of Glory.* It follows another work, *On Whose Authority?* They both have to do with the Holy Spirit, His gifts, and His power. Both are needed in this confusing age.

This book is vintage Charles Carrin.

Again and again, with precision and spiritual logic, he slams home the truth of the objective work and the subjective relationship of the Holy Spirit to the believer and church. His graphic experience with the Holy Spirit in being blasted from legalism to life is anchored by his expert exposition of the Scriptures. His straightforward dealing with the issues of grace and the gifts of the Spirit is most helpful as well as clarifying. I found Chapter 3 most useful in his differentiation and comparison of grace (*charis*), anointing (*chrios* and *chrisma*), gift (*charisma*), gifts (*charismata*) and Christ (*Christos*).

This work, seriously read and sincerely applied, will very likely bring its reader to a new level of awareness as well as usefulness. I am happy to commend it to your deepest interest and plan to continue to recommend it wherever I go.

—JACK TAYLOR
DIMENSIONS MINISTRIES
MELBOURNE, FLORIDA

Jack Taylor is former vice president of the Southern Baptist Convention, an ordained minister for more than fifty years, and a widely acclaimed conference speaker. The author of thirteen books, with 750,000 copies in circulation, he has traveled extensively around the world, preaching in SBC mission stations. Today his ministry is challenging believers of every denomination to a deeper, truer acceptance of the Holy Spirit's complete works.

Foreword

Charles Carrin is "America's best kept secret," says Dr. Jack Taylor. I agree. This book will help you to see why this is true. In these pages you will meet a man who has not had a high profile in his own country, yet in spite of this, he has managed to have an extraordinary ministry all over America.

In my twenty-five years at Westminster Chapel there are only three or four men who have impressed me so much that I was willing to put my reputation on the line in order to have them speak for us. Charles Carrin is one of those. I met him at a conference where both of us were speakers in Chattanooga, Tennessee. I was deeply moved when I heard him speak. It had been years since such an impact had been made on me by anyone. I asked to spend time with him, and an instantaneous relationship developed. I immediately began to think of how I could have him at Westminster Chapel. I returned to England and told our deacons about Charles. They were fascinated because they knew that I didn't get excited about anybody all that often. I asked the deacons to listen to the tape of the sermon that had so moved me, and there was a feeling that, indeed, we should invite him to Westminster Chapel.

We did. He came to us in October 2000, and he turned us upside-down—unlike anything we had seen in many years. He left a deposit of glory and of the presence of God that has made us a Spirit church as well as a Word church. I had been saying for years that the Word and the

Spirit need to come together, and yet I knew in my heart that Westminster Chapel—up until then—was mostly a Word church.

Perhaps I should explain. It seems to me that a silent divorce has taken place between the Word and the Spirit in the church. When there is a divorce, sometimes the children stay with the mother, sometimes the children stay with the father. In this divorce that is in the church, there are those who have stayed on the Word side and those who are on the Spirit side. What is the difference? Take the emphasis. Those who are on the Word side emphasize the need for preaching, knowing your doctrine, getting back to the doctrines of the Reformation, and expository ministry. What is wrong with such an emphasis? Absolutely nothing. What about those on the Spirit side—what are they saying? They are saying the need of the hour is to see signs, wonders, and miracles; we need to see power as in the Book of Acts, or the world will take no notice of the church; we need to see the gifts of the Spirit in operation. What is wrong with that emphasis? Absolutely nothing.

The need of the hour is for a remarriage of both the Word and the Spirit. I am happy to say that Charles Carrin combines both simultaneously in his ministry, and I doubt there are many people on either side of the Atlantic who could have had the impact upon Westminster Chapel as he did. This is partly because of his background, partly because of his gentle personality, and partly because we were ready for such a ministry.

This book will give you an idea of what I have tried to say above. It will introduce someone to the gifts of the Spirit who has a background, like myself, that is reformed and committed to the sovereignty of God. It will help others to see how one can believe in the sovereignty of God and also the gifts of the Spirit.

You won't be able to put this book down, and I pray that it will bless you and your friends and bring great honour and glory to the name of God.

−R.T. KENDALL
WESTMINSTER CHAPEL, LONDON
JANUARY 2001

Dr. R.T. Kendall was born on July 13, 1935, in Ashland, Kentucky. He is a graduate of Trevecca Nazarene College (A.B.), University of Louisville (M.A.), and Southern Baptist Theological Seminary (M.Div). In 1973, he went to England to do research in theology at Oxford University and received the D.Phil. in 1976. The following year, he became the minister of Westminster Chapel, London, following in the tradition of G. Campbell Morgan and Martyn Lloyd-Jones. He is the author of thirty books, including *The Anointing, The Sensitivity of the Spirit* and *God Meant It For Good*. He and his wife, Louise, have two children.

Preface

The primary purposes of this book are:

- To lead you into an encounter with the Holy Spirit that will revolutionize your life and ministry.

- To help you understand that the charismatic gifts of the Spirit are additional revelations of His grace.

- To clarify basic principles about the work of the Holy Spirit and to assist your becoming a more competent teacher of His Word.

- To provide brief highlights of Christian history that will make you aware of the Holy Spirit's willingness to use believers like yourself.

- To instruct and encourage you in your ministry to impart the power of the Holy Spirit to others through the laying-on of your hands.

Introduction

After the ascension of Jesus when the disciples went "everywhere preaching the word" (Acts 8:4) and were accused of "turning the world upside down" (Acts 17:6), they experienced the "powers of the age to come" (Heb. 6:5). They were no longer mere men and women; they became disciples under the anointing of the Holy Spirit. In a sense, they stood in the edge of glory. Their feet were on earth, but their faces were in heaven. Eternity shone through them like sunlight through a window.

Whether then or now, nothing is more astonishing than discovering that God has placed within reach of ordinary believers the amazing power of the Holy Spirit. That is precisely what Jesus has made available to us all. Through miraculous signs and wonders (for lack of better language, we call these "gifts of the Holy Spirit"), the Holy Spirit draws back the veil and allows us to actually experience His awesome power.

But the great tragedy of contemporary preaching is that many believers are taught about the Holy Spirit without being brought into a life-changing encounter with Him. Let us now embrace and enjoy all that God has for the church! He has promised us:

"Jesus stood and cried out, saying, 'If anyone thirsts, let him come to Me and drink. He who believes in Me, as the Scripture has said, out of his heart will flow rivers of living water.' But this He spoke concerning the Spirit, whom those believing in Him would receive; for the Holy Spirit was not yet given, because Jesus was not yet glorified" (Jn. 7:37–39).

"You shall receive power when the Holy Spirit has come upon you; and you shall be witnesses to Me..." (Acts 1:8).

"And with great power the apostles gave witness to the resurrection of the Lord Jesus. And great grace was upon them all" (Acts 4:33).

"For the kingdom of God is not in word but in power" (1 Cor. 4:20).

"My speech and my preaching were not with persuasive words of human wisdom, but in demonstration of the Spirit and of power, that your faith should not be in the wisdom of men but in the power of God" (1 Cor. 2:4–5).

"But you have an anointing from the Holy One, and you know all things... But the anointing which you have received from Him abides in you..." (1 Jn. 2:20, 27).

Chapter One

How It All Began

My wife, Laurie, was involved in a devastating automobile wreck while I was pastor of a congregation in Atlanta, Georgia. She was left with thirteen broken bones, multiple fractures, a collapsed lung and concussion of the brain. For forty days she remained hospitalized in a near-death condition.

That was the physical aspect of the tragedy. The spiritual aspect was that for a month before the accident occurred, I had a premonition it was going to happen. That terrifying knowledge plagued me constantly, dogged my heels, plunged me into such anguish I could not sleep at night. I prayed. I wept. I begged God not to do it. But my wife knew nothing about the distressing message, and I dared not tell her.

When the wreck occurred on July 29, 1977, I was two hundred miles from home, conducting the funeral of a friend. At the exact moment of the collision, I raised my wrist, looked at my watch, and my mind strangely photographed the setting of the hands on the dial: 12 noon. I was perplexed. A feeling of strangeness settled over me. Somehow I sensed "this is a significant moment."

When I returned home late that day, I found a note on the living room floor from the hospital, instructing me to report there immediately. I rushed to my wife's bedside, and as I stood there it seemed the devil himself was laughing at me, saying, "You knew it would happen. You even knew when it happened—today at 12:00 noon. But you were powerless to stop it!"

Nothing in my twenty-seven years of Christian ministry had prepared me for this.

No Room in My Theology

My first pastorate began on New Year's Eve, 1949, when I shoved my suitcases onto the vestibule of a train going from Miami to Atlanta. As we pulled out of the station, I was numb with fear. At age nineteen I had just been ordained to the ministry and was now stepping into a life that seemed totally overwhelming. There was no doubt God had called me to preach—but the responsibility awaiting me was frightening.

An emotional storm pounded my heart. While I was willing to serve God, deep inside I felt that I was missing something vital that would help me. Whatever that unknown factor was, I knew it could not be supplied by the church and university where I was heading. Nor did I know where to find it. Those I asked seemed not to understand my question.

Riding the full length of Florida that night, I stayed awake, thinking about the significance of this ride. I not only had gotten on the train in one year and would be getting off in the next, 1950, but I also had started my ride in the first half of the century and would be ending it in the last. As we rumbled through the dark Florida countryside, a more astonishing thought came to me. This was the final half-century of the millennium. When it closed, a new thousand-year period would be dawning.

The prophetic aspect of that fact gripped my mind. God had already forewarned me that a radical change lay hidden in my future. That thought also troubled me. But I could never have imagined that in the next fifty years evangelical Christianity would begin a revolutionary—and often painful—restoration to truths about the Holy Spirit it had rejected for centuries.

Along with my denomination, I believed the age of miracles had permanently ended; gifts of the Spirit surely had vanished with the death of the apostle John. We were ultra-conservative with no room in our theology for anything miraculous. Though certain scriptures regarding the Holy Spirit made me question our position, I had confidence we were right. With that assurance, I leaned back against the train seat, perhaps a little pridefully, feeling that doctrinally we were more correct than others.

My ordination had been on Christmas Day, and I vividly recalled the moment I knelt before a presbytery in Miami for the laying-on-of-hands. That had been an awesome event, but, according to my mentors, they had not bestowed any gift of the Holy Spirit upon me. However, they did examine me on my denomination's articles of faith. The first said: "We believe the Scripture of the Old and New Testament to be the inspired Word of God and the only rule of faith and practice." I found great security in those words; they said what my heart believed.

Yes, I loved the Scripture, and to my understanding, believed it totally. In my wildest imagination, I could never have foreseen the day when I would defy the churches I loved in defending 1 Corinthians 12 and 14 as "the inspired Word of God." That night on the train, had I known the Holy Spirit would make that demand in my future, I would have been even more terrified.

Thus, for the first twenty-seven years of ministry, I continued a course of traditional preaching, undergirding my orthodoxy with study at Columbia Presbyterian Seminary. God was wonderfully gracious to me and my congregations in those years, though the ministry remained powerless. In nearly three decades, I never saw one alcoholic, suicidal, drug addict, homosexual, Satanist, or any other person with such life-destroying compulsions miraculously delivered by the power of the Holy Spirit. It did not happen. Nor did I expect it to. My remedy for these problems was secular therapy—not Jesus. In my theology, the Holy Spirit verified the gospel and regenerated the unsaved. On every other human need He had closed the door.

My years of comfortable ministry ended as I wept and prayed next to the battered body of my wife in that hospital bed. I knew I needed a God who did more than what my theology taught. But I would be on the brink of suicide before I was humble enough to submit to what He said.

Meeting My Ananias

The next three months proved a terrorizing struggle of life and death for both my wife and me. My panic was compounded because of a sense of overwhelming, utter defeat. I knew only one thing: something dark and sinister was in control of our lives, and I was powerless to stop it. My pastor-friends had no explanations for the bizarre psychic premonition that had come to pass. We had no doctrines that ventured into such areas. As far as I knew, no one did. Physically, spiritually, and emotionally, I sank deeper into nightmarish depression. I had come to the end of three decades of pastoral work broken and defeated. My life and ministry had collapsed in total failure.

Laurie finally came home, facing months in a wheelchair, while I continued to scream at God for answers. Physically, she began to recover. Mentally, however, neither of us improved. Instead, my depression worsened, moving me steadily toward suicide. This represented a total personality change, for I had always been a happy, fun-loving person. Now, that abruptly ended. In total despair one day, I drove out the Stone Mountain Freeway, floored the accelerator, took both hands off the wheel, and screamed at God, "What are You going to do about it?"

How I survived that defiant act, I do not know. I have no further recollection of that drive. But a flicker of hope came weeks later when a gentle, inner voice spoke to me, "Here in Atlanta you will meet your Ananias." Who that would be, I did not know. How we would meet and what he would do, remained a mystery. I only knew that Saul of Tarsus' blindness ended when Ananias entered his life.

Soon afterward, a friend asked if I would visit an inmate in the Atlanta Federal Penitentiary. He knew little about the prisoner, except that, as he put it, "He is different." So began a series of visits with one of the most remarkable Christians I had ever met. In our early meetings he explained that the year before, in the Federal Penitentiary at Fort Leavenworth, Kansas, while in the act of attempted suicide, he had been miraculously born-again, delivered from depression, and filled with the Holy Spirit. Later he was transferred to Atlanta where our contact began.

At first I feared his spirituality. There was an aura about him I had never sensed on anyone before. He had every reason to be in despair. But he wasn't. Instead, he seemed to glow with a joy I had never seen or known. When he prayed, I felt peace, like a fragrance, move into his gloomy dungeon. He shared private information with me about things happening in my life that only God and I knew. He also prayed for patients in the prison hospital, and they were healed. He then led them to the Lord. Once an angry prisoner slapped his face and sneered, "Turn the other cheek, Christian!" and he did exactly that. Later the same prisoner returned repentant and asked forgiveness. I did not know what this unusual Christian had, but I knew I needed it.

On three separate occasions, while waiting for him in the visitors' room, I silently read Bible passages that spoke powerfully about my own crisis. To my amazement, when he came in he would open his Bible and read the same scriptures back to me, explaining their message in a spiritual depth I had never heard. Over and over, God revealed Himself through my friend. One day while this was happening, I again heard the voice inside me say, "Listen to what he has to say, Charles. He has your answer."

In a very gentle, but indisputable way, the prisoner showed me Bible passages regarding a work of the Holy Spirit about which I knew nothing—the "baptism in the Spirit." This experience, he explained, released the Spirit's miraculous works in believers. Though I was totally ignorant on the subject, I still drew back in fear. He persisted. No one had ever confronted my rejection of these scriptures before.

He even made scriptural sense of the strange psychic ordeal that my wife and I had been through. Carefully he explained the reality of two spiritual realms—good and evil. I soon admitted that I knew nothing about "gifts" of the Holy Spirit, the reality of demons, spiritual warfare, or the Scriptures' warning against sorcery (see Isaiah 47:11–12). As a teenager I had been exposed to levitation, Ouija boards, ESP (extrasensory perception), and had been vulnerable to other occult influences. Until now, no one had ever warned me of the spiritual danger in those practices.

In nearly ten thousand sermons, I never devoted one message to the subject of resisting Satan. Had anyone tried to talk to me about it, I would probably have dismissed him as a fanatic. Like many other pastors, I was insulated from learning anything that did not bear the mark of denominational approval. As a result, my wife and I were easy prey for the powers of darkness. My having "authority to trample on serpents and scorpions, and over all the power of the enemy" (Luke 10:19) or being "able to stand against the wiles of the devil" (Eph. 6:11) were ideas totally foreign to me.

Point by point, my prisoner friend lovingly presented truth. Admitting this is painful, but it was the truth that terrified me. My denomination closed its pulpits to all who believed in these strange doctrines about baptism and gifts of the Holy Spirit. If these things were true, and if I said yes to them, it meant the loss of my church, my house, my retirement, my friends, and everything I had worked thirty years to achieve. The decision I faced had tremendous repercussions. With that prospect before me, my depression grew worse. Fiercely so.

Saying Yes

God was unrelenting. He, not the prisoner, continued to press truth upon me. He demanded I accept every Bible verse regarding the work of the Holy Spirit. Somehow, I couldn't turn loose. Summer passed into an autumn of sleeplessness and hellish depression. Finally, one November day I went to the prison at the absolute bottom of despair.

As I sat across the table from my prisoner friend,

something inside me exploded. In an act of desperate surrender, I cried out "Yes!," bowed my head down on the table, and waited there trembling. In the same way Ananias must have laid hands on Saul of Tarsus in Damascus, the young man in olive-drab reached across the table and placed his hand on my head. It was an incredible moment. I was a pastor with nearly thirty years experience in ministry; he was newly saved. I was battling severe depression; he was glowing in the joy of the Lord. With a quiet, authoritative voice, he quoted Ananias' words to me: "The Lord Jesus, who appeared to you on the road as you came, has sent me that you may receive your sight and be filled with the Holy Spirit" (Acts 9:17).

With Mafia inmates and their girlfriends watching, the visitors' room in the Atlanta Georgia Federal Penitentiary became my house on the "street called Straight" (Acts 9:11). Just as God honored that ancient laying-on-of-hands, He honored this one.

The effect of that moment still defies description. Within minutes after I returned home I had an encounter with the Holy Spirit that permanently, wonderfully, revolutionized my life. The spirit of suicide was snatched out of me like dirty roots from the ground. I felt it go. Anger, rejection, psychic phenomena, crushing feelings of inferiority that had haunted me since childhood were yanked out.

The next moment, I felt as if I were standing under a spiritual Niagara Falls being filled by the power of God. Like a flood, the Holy Spirit overwhelmed me, plunging me out of sight into an ocean of His grace and love. For a while, I lay still, fearful to move, afraid that the glory of heaven that had fallen upon me would somehow vanish. I did not know what to call it at the time, but I was "under the power of the Holy Spirit." Where depression had forced me down, I now felt weightless, suspended, as if in a cloud. That day, with totally new meaning, I experienced the "Scripture as the inspired Word of God and my only rule of faith."

The blessing I wish had happened before my ordination and that train ride to my first church in 1949 finally took place.

Caught Up in Love for Jesus

My new love for Jesus was so overwhelming that for several years I never read a newspaper, watched television or did many things that formerly had been normal for me. It was not that I disciplined myself in that way; there was no self-effort in it. Nothing could replace my devotion for Jesus. He simply became my "all in all."

The months that passed were a time of intense love-relationship with Him; so much so that I wanted to hug everyone I met, tell them about the wonderful power of the Holy Spirit, and acknowledge "every good thing which is in [me] in Christ Jesus" (Philem. 6). For the first time in nearly thirty years of preaching, I truly understood the bride's longing for her groom in the Song of Solomon: "My beloved spoke, and said to me: 'Rise up, my love, my fair one, and come away. For lo, the winter is past, the rain is over and gone. The flowers appear on the earth; the time of singing has come, and the voice of the turtledove is heard in our land'" (Song of Sol. 2:10–12).

My dark winter of depression had forever ended. Flowers sprouted everywhere. God's beauty surrounded me. Once, while praying in the woods, I opened my eyes to see every leaf and limb, grass blade and stone, glistening like polished silver. Where in those same woods earlier, I heard only my own groaning, I now heard the Lord's voice in carefully spoken "words of knowledge." These were words about people and circumstances which were later exactly fulfilled. For months I had suffered from insomnia; now I slept in deep, deep peace. Jesus had kept His promise: The Comforter had come.

In time, my wife fully recovered. She and our daughter Cecile experienced their own wonderful renewals in the Holy Spirit and joined me in an exciting new ministry. We emerged from our hellish ordeal having learned "the way of God more accurately" (Acts 18:26). Thankfully, we realized that powers of darkness had caused the wreck. It was not God. We also learned to "submit to God. Resist the devil and he will flee from you" (James 4:7). Depression and suicide never returned.

The Great Adventure

Astonishingly, within a short time, miraculous "signs and wonders" suddenly appeared in my ministry. Gifts of the Spirit my friend had told me about began operating. One of my former church members who had been an alcoholic for eighteen years and whom I had never been able to help was delivered in a few minutes time. She never drank again. Drug addicts, homosexuals, suicidals, alcoholics and others like them were transformed. I was amazed. People were healed. Other pastors came for ministry and were blessed. The scene of Philip's ministry in Samaria became commonplace. Without my trying, "Unclean spirits, crying with a loud voice, came out of many" (Acts 8:7–8).

A young woman whose father was in the Baseball Hall of Fame was freed from addiction and her family saved. I remember the first person who was overcome by the power of the Spirit after I prayed for him. He was a fellow Calvinistic pastor. When I prayed, lightly touching him, he slumped unconscious to the floor. I was more shocked than he, but he rose from the experience with new revelation about his ministry.

That was only the beginning. Many times afterward the presence of the Holy Spirit would be so strong that when I hugged people leaving church, they dropped under the power of God. In this unexpected display of His presence, God spoke to them, healed them and filled them with His glory. Remarkably to me all this was happening to one who had been a hard-line unbeliever in the Holy Spirit's miraculous signs and wonders.

Seemingly, I had the poorest credentials possible for such a radical change of ministry. But, like the father rushing out to meet the prodigal son, God threw His arms around me. The robe He put on me was a mantle of power; the ring, a sign of covenant love (see Luke 15:22). On my feet were the sandals of peace (see Ephesians 6:15). From that astonishing day at the penitentiary, under the hands of an imprisoned Ananias, I began the greatest adventure of my life.

The Holy Spirit in My Church

Within two years after my friend laid hands on me and I was filled with the Holy Spirit, I saw more people changed by the power of God than in all my previous twenty-seven years as a pastor. Since then, I have witnessed men and women from all walks of life transformed by an encounter with the Holy Spirit. Some were physicians, college professors, pastors, street people, airline pilots, famous athletes, skilled professionals, children and the elderly. They can verify that their lives were radically turned around by the power of God. But rather than give my opinion about the effects of their encounters with the Holy Spirit and the change He brought, they can speak for themselves.

One of them is a woman who was skeptical about visible demonstrations of the Holy Spirit. She wrote:

11

Let me tell you about the awesome and powerful way God touched me in a service you held at Christ Chapel in the summer of 1993. I had only known Jesus for a few months and had never been in a meeting where the Holy Spirit moved with signs and wonders. I had never been knocked to the floor by the power of God, and I simply did not believe in such things.

The year before, three discs in my neck were ruptured, and my arm became numb. X-rays and an MRI not only confirmed the ruptured discs but also showed that the nerve which went to my right arm had been deprived of blood so long it was now dead. The doctor explained that even surgery would not help, and in time, probably the arm would atrophy. The pain in my back was constant, and there was very little feeling left in my fingertips. I could not even pick up my Bible or open doors with my right hand.

Then one night when you came down the aisle toward the pulpit, you stopped at the row where I was standing and pointed at me. You had an usher bring me out. I was frightened and determined I was not going to fall. But when you touched my shoulders I felt a power, a force, an energy, like I had never come in contact with before, and I fell. You said, simply "She's Yours, Holy Spirit."

I couldn't believe this was happening to me. I wondered, *Could this possibly be God?* Then, I sensed a small, quiet "feeling" deep within me urging me not to move. But, I thought, *There is no way I am going to lie here and be humiliated.* So I got up and went back to my seat.

Within a minute you came back and pointed to me again. When I stepped out you said with an urgency: "Now, please! Receive everything God has for you!"

And again I was on the floor. This time I knew it was God, and His power was on me. As I lay there, I humbled myself and asked Him to forgive me for getting up before. I told Him I would lie there as long as He wanted me to, and that I wanted all He had for me.

Then I felt a surge of power moving in my body. It was like velvet-covered electrical currents. It moved down my spine to the very end, then came back up again. Next, it went down my right arm and back up. It did this over and over again.

I don't know how long I lay with the hand of God touching deep inside my body. But I was so filled with joy because now I knew God is not only alive but He still touches and talks to us today. It wasn't until I got home that I discovered I was healed. Totally.

That horrible, agonizing pain has never returned to my neck or back. I have written this entire letter with my right hand! My right arm continues to work perfectly. I give all praise and glory to Jesus! He has made me whole! He has set my feet upon the solid Rock. Glory, honor, and power to His holy name!

—Rose Smith
Florence, Alabama

In the first half of my ministry, such a letter would have been unthinkable. Today, it is one of many that testify to the healing power of Jesus. Though I regard myself as an ordinary minister with few special talents, there is no way I can deny the number of people whose lives have been radically changed by the Holy Spirit. It has happened. And it has been He, the Holy Spirit, not me.

My advice to every believer, especially pastors, is this: Seek the Holy Spirit! With all your heart, go after God. Let nothing hinder you from receiving the Spirit's mighty empowering! This is the "Promise of the Father" (Acts 1:4). When He comes upon you, anointing you, it will be that imparting—and only that imparting—that "breaks the yoke" of bondage. That wonderful experience heals, delivers, normalizes and sets men free (see Isaiah 10:27). But how does one receive that imparting? Jesus Himself is your example. He too received the "anointing" (Luke 4:16–21). In the next chapter we will see how it happened to Him, the changes it brought and how it can also happen to you.

Chapter Two

Anointing: The Fragrance of Jesus

S piritually, we have only two choices: we either smell like resurrection or like a corpse. Denominational membership has nothing to do with it. From beginning to end, relationship with Jesus releases the power of the Holy Spirit.

The Original Apostles and the Anointing

On the day of the Resurrection, Jesus suddenly appeared in the closed room where the disciples had gathered. He "breathed on them, and said to them, 'Receive the Holy Spirit'" (John 20:22). In that phenomenal moment, each one received the life-changing, regenerating power of God. That day, they were born-again, permanently transformed, translated from the dispensation of law into the dispensation of grace. In a moment's time, they stepped from the old covenant into the new. The new birth was exclusively a new covenant provision; it was foretold in the old but became reality only when the Resurrection had become historic fact.

Exciting as this new birth was for the disciples, an equally dramatic imparting of the Holy Spirit awaited them. While they were still rejoicing over the Resurrection, Jesus "commanded them not to depart from Jerusalem, but to wait for the Promise of the Father... He said... You shall be baptized with the Holy Spirit not many days from now... You shall receive power when the Holy Spirit has come upon you; and you shall be witnesses to Me in Jerusalem, and in all Judea and Samaria, and to the end of the earth" (Acts 1:4–5, 8).

It is vital that we recognize the difference in these two impartings of the Spirit. The first achieved the disciples' personal salvation; the second, at Pentecost, was for empowering their ministry. As I will show in detail later, this followed the exact pattern of Jesus' two experiences with the Holy Spirit: conception and anointing.

We might assume the disciples' three years of ministry-training under Jesus, their love for Him, and their receiving the Holy Spirit on the day of the Resurrection, prepared them for power-endued ministry. Not so. These men would not be totally prepared to cast out demons, heal the sick or relieve the oppressed until the Holy Spirit had come "upon" them. Jesus' most urgent instruction on the Mount of Ascension was that they not leave Jerusalem but wait for "the Promise of the Father" (Luke 24:49; Acts 1:4). This expression, "Promise of the Father," is a specific reference to the ministry-power of the Holy Spirit (see Acts 2:33).

While Pentecost was another new covenant provision and an additional confirmation of Jesus' resurrection, it did not come simultaneously with the disciples' new birth. Rather it came in fulfillment of that "Promise of the Father," of which we later read: "When the Day of Pentecost had fully come... they were all filled with the Holy Spirit" (Acts

2:1–4). After the Resurrection Jesus was seen by five hundred brethren at one time (see 1 Corinthians 15:6), yet on the Day of Pentecost, only 120 were in the Upper Room. At least 380 missed the Holy Spirit's outpouring.

Thankfully, in days following, thousands more were baptized in the Holy Spirit. The point is this: Today, as then, not all saved people experience their personal "Promise of the Father." However, historians estimate that within fifty-six years following the outpouring of the Holy Spirit, the gospel had been preached throughout the Roman world, much of the Far East, and quickly reached the British Isles.

Jesus' Anointing Is Your Example

Now let's look at the two impartings of the Spirit in Jesus' life, for His experience is our model.

The first imparting of the Spirit was when Jesus was conceived in the womb of the Virgin by the Holy Spirit (Luke 1:34–35). The second imparting occurred thirty years later at the introduction of His public ministry (Luke 4:16–19). These two are very definite and essential works of the Spirit in Jesus' experience. One could not replace the other.

Let's compare these two anointings. Conception by the Spirit occurred in the womb (Luke 1:31–35). Anointing by the Spirit occurred in the Jordan River (Luke 3:21–22). The first incarnated Him into human flesh and prepared Him for the cross, atonement and redemption. The second made Him Messiah and equipped Him for kingdom ministry of miracles and healing.

The Hebrew word *Messiah* and the Greek word *Christ* both mean "Anointed One." They are not references to His incarnation. In the synagogue of Nazareth, Jesus explained, "The Spirit of the LORD is upon Me, because He has anointed Me to preach... to heal... to deliver... to recover sight... to liberate..." (see Luke 4:18). The key is the word *upon*. In this instance, Jesus referred only to the Spirit's descent upon Himself in the Jordan River; He made no reference to what happened in the womb. In that brief message in Nazareth, He showed that anointing and ministry are inseparably connected. His anointing, like that of Aaron, David, Solomon, kings, priests and others, was for kingdom ministry.

Note how these two facts clearly define the Holy Spirit's dual work in Jesus:

1. The Spirit's work of incarnation destined Jesus to the cross and provided redemption for mankind (see Ephesians 2:16; Colossians 2:14).

2. The Spirit's anointing upon Jesus verified the presence of His kingdom on earth (see Matthew 12:28).

The anointing is the only part of the Holy Spirit's work that Jesus offers us. When He said, "He who believes in Me, the works that I do he will do also; and greater works than these he will do" (John 14:12), He was speaking of the anointing, not the cross. It is important to recognize this truth: Gifts of the Spirit draw back the veil, allowing us to experience the "powers of the age to come" (Heb. 6:5) and see the glory that waits beyond this present life. That revelation makes faith possible in those who otherwise have difficulty believing.

The cry from Calvary, "My God! My God! Why have You forsaken Me?" occurred because the anointing lifted from Him. Now, the Helper was gone. The removal of the Spirit at crucifixion did not affect Jesus' incarnation as the Son of God. Everything given Him at conception remained; only what came upon Him in the Jordan River left at the cross.

Nor is that departure to be confused with Jesus' cry to

the Father, "Into Your hands I commit My spirit" (Luke 23:46). As true man, Jesus possessed spirit, soul, and body. His spirit, which He committed to the will of the Father, descended to Sheol (see 1 Peter 3:18–20); His soul, (the life of which is in the blood, Leviticus 17:11), was "poured out... unto death" (Isa. 53:12). His physical body was laid in Joseph's new tomb (see John 19:40–42). Scripture carefully details these three aspects of His death.

Why the Removal of the Comforter Was Necessary

As the ultimate scapegoat, Jesus had to be abandoned to die (see Leviticus 16:10).

His personal ministry of preaching, healing, delivering, had ended. The need for the anointing was gone (see John 16:10).

The Holy Spirit lifted from Jesus' earthly human body in anticipation of anointing Jesus' new body–the church–on the Day of Pentecost (Acts 1:4–8).

The Extension of Jesus' Power

Before Pentecost, Jesus "called His twelve disciples together and gave them power and authority over all demons, and to cure diseases" (Luke 9:1). The key word is "together." Jesus did not find John at the Jordan, Matthew at the Mediterranean, Peter in Galilee and confer power upon them separately. He called them together. Though they ministered two by two, their anointing remained part of the original whole that was on Jesus. Later, at Pentecost, each of them received personal anointings.

In our day, the anointing still works as one indivisible provision for the entire body of Christ. Those who wish to function in the anointing must be willing to minister to the whole body. God will not sustain the anointing in those who promote division. All born-again parts must be willing to accept all other born-again parts. It was unity of heart, not uniformity of style, for which Jesus prayed. The first disciples maintained personal originality. So may we. A contrived religious conformity has proved to be as deadly to the kingdom as disunity. Jesus prayed "that they all may be one, as You, Father, are in Me, and I in You; that they also may be one in Us, that the world may believe that You sent Me" (John 17:21).

Unity among the disciples of Christ must precede the world's believing. Paul exposed the destructive results of disunity within the church when he wrote that failure in "discerning the Lord's body" caused many to be "weak and sick among you, and many sleep" (1 Cor. 11:30). In this passage, the apostle refers primarily to discerning the Lord's body in the communion service. The principle applies, however, to every other aspect involving the body of Jesus. Whether in the Lord's Supper or in His corporate-presence in other believers, the end result for failing to acknowledge Him is the same: "Many are weak and sick among you, and many sleep."

Tragically, some believers place greater value on defending division than on promoting restoration. In doing so, they destroy themselves. Isolationism is always deadly. Logic and Scripture verify this fact.

One horse can sled-pull one thousand pounds. Two horses can pull six thousand pounds. By cooperating with another, each horse increases his output three hundred percent. Larger teams produce accelerated power. Eighty-five percent of all results, good or bad, come from the efforts of the group. They do not come from individual effort.

God's principle declares that "one [believer shall] chase a thousand, and two put ten thousand to flight" (Deut. 32:30).

By flying in a "V" formation, geese add 71 percent greater flying range than if each goose flew alone. That's because the flight pattern creates an aeronautical uplift that benefits each bird behind the leader. Christians who isolate themselves, refusing to fly in formation with others, reveal their insecurity, immaturity, and lack of discretion. Don't do it.

Elijah demonstrated the power-in-unity principle during his contest with the prophets of Baal on Mount Carmel. Scripture says Elijah chose to make his offering at the "time of the... evening sacrifice" (1 Kings 18:36). The "evening sacrifice" refers to the sacrifice that was taking place on the great altar in Jerusalem eighty miles away from where Elijah was making his offering on the mountain. Daily in the Holy City a lamb was offered as a morning and evening sacrifice (see Exodus 29:38–46). By observing the sunset, Elijah knew the moment when the priests at the temple would be making their offering to God; he then timed his sacrifice on Mount Carmel to coincide with theirs.

Key Point:

Elijah drew upon the release of kingdom-power taking place in Jerusalem. By uniting himself with priests in the Holy City, he fortified his own ministry a thousand-fold.

Elijah's story has another twist from a New Testament perspective. In New Testament language, Jerusalem symbolizes heaven. So Elijah was doing what Jesus described in Matthew 18:18: "Binding on earth... binding in heaven... loosing on earth... loosing in heaven." In that inviolate

21

union with God and the priests in Jerusalem, he could not be defeated. Identically, the church today must draw upon the anointing which is on the whole body of Christ. The power of that unity is inestimable. Jesus said, "Again I say to you that if two of you agree on earth concerning anything that they ask, it will be done for them by My Father in heaven" (Matt. 18:19).

This is not an invitation to casual agreement. Not at all. For instance, the word *agree* in the Greek text is *sumphoneo* and can also be translated as "symphonize." The word denotes harmony in the highest spiritual order. Thus, when Balaam, a sorcerer and witch doctor, came to Moab to curse Israel, his evil intention never took place. As he looked down from the top of Mount Pisgah at a place called Peor, Balaam "saw Israel encamped according to their tribes; and the Spirit of God came upon him" (Num. 24:2).

Study this fact carefully: The Spirit's descent on this pagan prophet was not in response to Israel's prayer for deliverance or God's sudden decision to protect them. Rather, prompting for the Spirit's descent came from a totally different source: It was Balaam's sight of Israel encamped "according to their tribes." Looking down, the pagan witch doctor saw godly order, spiritual harmony, a holy pattern, that projected power beyond everything he possessed.

Moreover, Balaam did not see people scattered about in self-chosen ways. He saw heaven-empowered unity— and his witchcraft was no match for it. The sight below was like a vacuum which drew the Spirit of God down upon him. A blessing for Israel poured out of Balaam's mouth involuntarily. Some of the greatest prophetic revelations of the Messiah and Israel came from this strange man. It was he who announced, "A Star shall come out of

Jacob; A Scepter shall rise out of Israel" (Num. 24:17). His prophecy brought wise men from the East to Bethlehem seeking one whose star identified the "King of the Jews." What Balaam saw from the mountains of Pisgah was power—power that overwhelmed his curse and forced a blessing upon the people of God.

In the same way, when Christians today lock arms, renounce division and submit to the solidarity for which Jesus prayed, even the occult, unbelieving world will be compelled to bless us. It cannot be otherwise. The power to prevent or to promote the curse lies within our own camp. By unity or disunity, we determine blessing or blasphemy. It is not decided by the witch doctor on the mountain. It rises from within. "He who is in you is greater than he who is in the world" (1 John 4:4).

If you want power in your life and ministry, be certain that your motivating factor is grace. Maintain a loving attitude toward the whole body of Christ. That does not mean you ignore sin or heresy. Rather it simply means that, like Jesus, you graciously love the sinner while you help him overcome his sin. You cannot correct anyone with whom you have no relationship. Attempting that is disastrous. Don't try it.

Banish the foolish notion that you are an independent arm or leg. There is no such thing. Unite yourself with total kingdom power as Elijah did. Recognize that pride and vanity are your greatest enemies. Humble yourself before someone else; ask for their spiritual inventory of you. If you need deliverance from a malevolent spirit, get it. Be honest. Be real. Be straightforward. Finally, with all your heart, seek the anointing. Be persistent!

Jesus said, "Everyone who asks receives" (Matt. 7:8). Go wherever the river of the Spirit is flowing. Plunge in. Drink. Get filled. Forget everything else. When you do, power will radiate from you like heat from an oven. Demons will leave at your command. You will become a true New Testament believer. Best of all, Jesus will be glorified, and the Father will say of you, "This is My beloved child in whom I am well pleased."

The Gift of the Spirit Provided

Scripture declares many times that God has provided believers with the gift of the Holy Spirit. These are the verses that the Lord led me to meditate on and accept when my life was so out of control. They are the inspired Word of God, and we cannot ignore them.

1. "I will pour out My Spirit on all flesh..." (Joel 2:28).

2. Jesus "will baptize you with the Holy Spirit..." (Luke 3:16).

3. "He who believes in Me... out of his heart will flow rivers of living water... He spoke concerning the Spirit..." (John 7:37–39).

4. "How much more will your heavenly Father give the Holy Spirit to those who ask Him?" (Luke 11:13).

5. "You shall receive power when the Holy Spirit has come upon you" (Acts 1:8).

6. "Repent... be baptized, ...and you shall receive the gift of the Holy Spirit. For the promise is to you and to your children" (Acts 2:38–39).

7. "We are His witnesses to these things, and so also is the Holy Spirit whom God has given to those who obey Him" (Acts 5:32).

8. "Our gospel did not come to you in word only, but also in power, and in the Holy Spirit and in much assurance" (1 Thess. 1:5).

9. "I will know, not the word of those who are puffed up, but the power. For the kingdom of God is not in word but in power" (1 Cor. 4:19–20).

The Spirit's Two-Fold Pattern: Salvation and Anointing

The Book of Acts identifies five groups who experienced salvation and anointing in separate phases. The 120 disciples at Pentecost were the first. Here are the others:

1. **The Samaritans.**

   Salvation: "Then Philip went down to the city of Samaria and preached Christ to them... But when they believed Philip as he preached the things concerning the kingdom of God and the name of Jesus Christ, both men and women were baptized" (Acts 8:5,12).

   Baptism in the Spirit: "Now when the apostles who were at Jerusalem heard that Samaria had received the word of God, they sent Peter and John to them, who, when they had come down, prayed for them that they might receive the Holy Spirit. For as yet He had fallen upon none of them... Then they laid hands on them, and they received the Holy Spirit" (Acts 8:14–17).

2. **Saul of Tarsus.**

   Salvation: "As he journeyed he came near Damascus, and suddenly a light shone around him from heaven. Then he fell to the ground, and heard a voice saying to him, 'Saul, Saul, why are you persecuting Me?' '...Who are You, Lord?...' 'I am Jesus'" (Acts 9:3–5).

   Baptism in the Spirit: "And Ananias went his way and entered the house; and laying his hands on him he said, 'Brother Saul, the Lord Jesus, who appeared to you on the road as you came, has sent me that you may receive your sight and be filled with the Holy Spirit'" (Acts 9:17).

3. **Cornelius.**

Salvation: "A devout man and one who feared God with all his household, who gave alms generously to the people, and prayed to God always... [the angel said], 'Your prayers and your alms have come up for a memorial before God'" (Acts 10:2, 4).

Baptism in the Spirit: "While Peter was still speaking these words, the Holy Spirit fell upon all those who heard the word... For they heard them speak with tongues and magnify God. Then Peter answered, 'Can anyone forbid water, that these should not be baptized who have received the Holy Spirit just as we have?'" (Acts 10:44–47).

4. **Ephesian Believers.**

Salvation: Paul "came to Ephesus. And finding some disciples he said to them, 'Did you receive the Holy Spirit when you believed?' So they said to him, 'We have not so much as heard whether there is a Holy Spirit'" (Acts 19:1–2).

Baptism in the Spirit: "When Paul had laid hands on them, the Holy Spirit came upon them, and they spoke with tongues and prophesied" (Acts 19:6).

Paul did not question the Ephesians' salvation; he did question their lack of power. Like many believers today, they had received the new birth but not the "Promise of the Father." Ephesus contained the greatest architectural wonder of the ancient world—the temple of Diana. Worshipers came to this site from every province of the Roman Empire. (See Acts 19:23–41.) As such, the city was a bastion of demonic activity.

The church in Ephesus had accomplished absolutely no growth, no victory over paganism. When Paul arrived he asked the all-revealing question, "Did you receive the Holy

Spirit when you believed?" (Acts 19:2). Their answer was, "No." And when Paul "laid hands on them, the Holy Spirit came upon them, and they spoke with tongues and prophesied." Immediately the power of God slammed upon the city in a way that broke curses, demolished demonic strongholds, and eventually emptied the world-famous temple. Ephesus then became one of the greatest Christian citadels in history. The anointing made the difference.

Key Point:

> Regeneration did not equip the Ephesian believers for their explosive success. Baptism in the Spirit did.

Bonding to Jesus

When Jesus called His disciples, He gave them four purposes.

> "Then He appointed twelve, that (1) they might be with Him and that (2) He might send them out to preach, and (3) to have power to heal sicknesses and (4) to cast out demons" (Mark 3:14–15, numbers added).

All four of these purposes relate directly to the anointing. The first was "that they might be with Him." Relationship with Jesus has priority over every other consideration; absolutely nothing excels it. The anointing is released through relationship with Him alone. The other three—preaching, healing and casting out demons—important as they are, are dependent upon our first being "with Him."

This bonding to Jesus also has a parallel in the Old Testament: "Moses went up to God, and the LORD called to him from the mountain, saying... 'I bore you on eagles' wings and *brought you to Myself*'" (Exod. 19:3–4). God's ultimate purpose for Israel was not the Promised Land, covenants, blessings or prosperity. His purpose was *to bring them to Himself*.

Identically, Barnabas and Saul were sent out by the church in Antioch when the Holy Spirit said, "Now separate *to Me* Barnabas and Saul for the work to which I have called them" (Acts 13:2). The first consideration was separation "to God." Commitment "to the work" was secondary. Believers whose first concern is their work or denominational membership, instead of God, and who reject relationship to the total body of Christ, will not function in the Holy Spirit's fullness. Whatever success they enjoy will be less than what it could have been.

We are all codependent on each other. An independent attitude produces spiritual leukemia in which one cell attacks another. This is hell's most effective warfare tactic against the church.

I am told that certain tribes of bees, when encountering bees from other tribes in the same flower, fight each other to the death. Moths, butterflies or ants in the same spot are not bothered by the bees. They only kill their own kind. Entomologists have determined that the bees' body odor is the offense. They do not like the smell of the other bee and try to destroy it.

These bees would have gone extinct long ago except for one key fact: Once a bee is covered with pollen and perfumed by the flower, its odor is no longer an annoyance to other bees. They then work peaceably, side by side. Paul wrote of this perfume principle in the Christian life:

> Now thanks be to God who always leads us in triumph in Christ, and through us diffuses the fragrance of His knowledge in every place. For we are to God the fragrance of Christ among those who are being saved and among those who are perishing. To the one we are the

aroma of death leading to death, and to the other the aroma of life leading to life (2 Cor. 2:14–16).

There is a very real application of this bee problem to the Christian walk. Some Christians buzz from one conflict to another. Their simple routine of living is difficult. They are quarrelsome, critical of others, self-defensive and quick to justify themselves. These folks blame everyone else for problems they create. Confronting them is not pleasant. They sting. We learn to avoid them. The situation sometimes requires us to stay out of the flowers. But avoiding the flowers robs our fellowship as Christian bees.

The answer for all of us is the same: We need to get fully covered with the sweetness of God's flower. That flower is Jesus. We are to

> "put off... the old man which grows corrupt according to the deceitful lusts, and be renewed in the spirit of your mind, and... put on the new man which was created... in true righteousness and holiness" (Eph. 4:22).

Someone asks, "How can I do that?" Fly to Christ! Get into the Flower! Become immediately occupied with making honey for the kingdom of God. Don't wait to see what other bees are doing. Be certain that you are covered with the fragrance of grace; put down your weapons of warfare and be conformed to Christ.

Key Point:

> The flower's perfume makes the difference; there is an unmistakable fragrance—beautiful, awesome, wonderful—to the resurrected life.

The bee who has reached the nectar of God's perfect will has little time for fighting his brothers and sisters. He has tasted the glory of God's love; in that simple taste he has been transformed. Old things have truly passed away, all things have become new. He now has a new peace with God, with himself and with others. The warfare has ended. His old body odor of carnal nature is gone. In its place is the new fragrance of a garden. Such a person has ceased from his self-works and stepped into rest with God.

The failure of many Christians is that they have spent too little time with Christ. They have busied themselves with religious things but still have not entered deeply into the resurrected life. It is in closeness with Christ that men and women become saints. The nearer we draw, the more heavy becomes the nectar's anointing. The richer the anointing is, the more powerful the Holy Spirit's outpouring from us. It is this outpouring of which Jesus spoke, "Out of his heart will flow rivers of living water" (John 7:38). This flowing out of the Spirit cannot happen if we are still fighting our own kind. Each of us must make our personal trip to the Flower and receive the anointing of the Holy Spirit. There is no other way but to be covered with the fragrance of God.

Had you been present at the garden tomb the morning of the Resurrection, though blind and deaf, you would still have known that Jesus had risen: You would have smelled fragrance from the open grave. His body had been anointed with more than one hundred pounds of aloe and spice (see John 19:39–40).

Likewise, had you been present at the Tabernacle of Moses, though blind and deaf, you would have known when worship was taking place by the smells. Had you been near Aaron, Zacharias or other priests when they came from the Tabernacle, you would have smelled the fragrance of God upon them.

The question is this: What do people smell when they get around you? Is it your own body odor or the fragrance of Christ? People who linger around the resurrection, smell like "myrrh and aloes" (John 19:39). This is the fragrance of anointing.

More than a millennium before the Resurrection, Solomon wrote about the Spirit's fragrance at the garden tomb. He said, "Awake, O north wind, and come, O south! Blow upon my garden, that its spices may flow out" (Song of Sol. 4:16). Our goal must be to experience that fragrance, not merely to operate in power. The search ends only when, like the woman with the box of spikenard, our own alabaster is broken and the fragrance of resurrection is released from us (see Mark 14:3). Then we can say with Paul: "I also count all things loss for the excellence of the knowledge of Christ Jesus my Lord... that I may gain Christ and be found in Him... *that I may know Him and the power of His resurrection*" (Phil. 3:8–10, emphasis added). This is Paul's way of saying that he wants to be totally covered with the sweetness of Jesus. It is the key to operating in the phenomenal power of the Holy Spirit.

Only two natures are identified with the anointing: the lamb nature and the dove nature. Scripture reveals this principle at Jesus' baptism: "The next day John saw Jesus coming toward him, and said, 'Behold! The Lamb of God who takes away the sin of the world!'" A moment after saying these words, "John bore witness, saying, 'I saw the Spirit descending from heaven like a dove, and He remained upon Him'" (John 1:29, 32).

This pattern is true for everyone who receives the anointing. The dove descends only upon a lamb. Arrogance, pride, egotism and self-will must go. Inward grace produces outward graciousness. Grace without character change is merely "sounding brass or a clanging cymbal" (1 Cor. 13:1). The character change that the

Holy Spirit seeks in us is the death of ego and pride. Where carnality still reigns, grace is unable to do its anointing work.

When the anointing is present, signs, wonders and gifts of healings may occur without the laying on of hands. This is a significant fact. Though Scripture speaks of laying on of hands, it does not say that is a requirement for the Spirit to move. God does not want us to focus on a formula of actions or words but on coming into His anointing. When we are in His presence, God can heal even if we are not seeking a healing. The following story illustrates this.

> In a downtown store I lost my balance. When I fell my arm went through a pair of hand trucks. Searing pain struck like nothing I had ever experienced. In the hospital emergency room, the doctors explained that I had a severely torn rotator cuff and had suffered an inverted dislocation of the shoulder. My shoulder was in a cast for nine weeks, and when it was removed the shoulder and elbow were frozen in position. After five months of therapy I could only lift my arm to the height of my shoulder. Doctors said that 30 percent movement was the most I could hope for.
>
> A year later, my husband and I heard that Charles Carrin was preaching at Christ Chapel in Florence. As a Baptist, I knew that healing today was only done through doctors. I went for the praise service. I remember during the message turning to my husband and telling him I was burning up with heat. After the sermon, Brother Carrin laid hands on many. I was one of them. Although I did not fall as many others did, again I felt the same flush of heat as before.
>
> After the service, we went to a restaurant with friends. At one point in our discussion I turned to a

friend, "Did I just lift my arm?" She replied she thought I had. Turning to my husband, I asked the same question, not daring to try. He wasn't sure. So I slowly lifted my arm straight up. I was healed. The doctors were completely astonished. Yes, God does heal today!"

—Sara Blankenship
Florence, Alabama

Chapter Three

The Holy Spirit's Charisma Gifts Are Available to You

One time when I was conducting a midweek prayer service, I received a very simple word of knowledge: "Pray for Mildred." It was as if I heard the words without my outer ear being involved. Even though the message was so clear, for a moment I was puzzled; but I proceeded to simply announce to those praying: "Pray for Mildred." The people continued praying. Moments later, I received a second instruction: "Mildred is Jewish." So I shared that information. As a result, members of the congregation sincerely prayed for this unknown Jewish lady named Mildred.

At the close of the service, a distinguished looking matron hurried down the aisle. In a breathy voice she said to me, "May I speak to the congregation?" I handed her the microphone.

"I have never addressed a church audience before," she explained, "but tonight I must. As a visitor I came because of a telephone call I received from a friend in Pennsylvania.

She and I were sorority sisters in college fifty years ago and have remained close friends ever since. Tonight she is seriously ill in the hospital, and she asked if I could find a church that would pray for her."

The woman paused, trying to maintain her composure, "This was the church I felt impressed to ask for prayer. I arrived too late to make the proper request in advance. But apparently that wasn't necessary because the Lord told you for me. You see, my friend's name is Mildred, and she is Jewish."

Later I learned the visitor went home, called her Jewish friend and told her what had happened. As a result Mildred was healed. Moreover, she was so impressed at how the Holy Spirit miraculously spoke her name and Jewish identity to our congregation more than a thousand miles away that she went to a Baptist church in her community, believed the gospel, and accepted Jesus Christ as her savior. Plainly, the Holy Spirit's gift of that evening revealed itself in a three-step progression: First, as a word of knowledge; second, as healing and finally, as salvation. Salvation is always the destination of grace.

The Meaning of Charisma

Nine different Greek words in the King James Version are translated as "gift." We will focus primarily on one—*charisma*—and its variations.

They are:

1. *Charis* — grace
2. *Chrios* — to anoint
3. *Chrisma* — the anointing itself
4. *Charisma* — the effects of the anointing
5. *Charismata* — plural of charisma
6. *Christos* — Christ; anointed one
7. *Christianos* — Christians; anointed ones

The Holy Spirit's Charisma Gifts Are Available to You

The apostle Paul wrote an eighty-four verse treatise on spiritual gifts (see 1 Corinthians 12–14) that provides the most comprehensive, authoritative information we have on the subject. More importantly, it is the only resource bearing the seal of divine authorship. All conflicting opinions, no matter how cherished or long-established, are but human speculation. *Scripture is our final, absolute authority.*

The apostle begins his dissertation with the plea: "Now concerning spiritual gifts, brethren, I do not want you to be ignorant" (12:1). Interestingly, this appeal that we "not be ignorant" appears seven times in the New Testament—once by Peter, six times by Paul. Each time the request reveals an especially deep concern of the writer. Its appearance here should command the attention of every conscientious believer.

The apostle proceeds carefully to detail the operation of nine grace works of the Spirit, concluding with the stirring rebuke, "But if anyone is ignorant, let him be ignorant" (14:38). In other words, he says, "After this careful explanation, if anyone refuses to learn, I have nothing more to say to him. Let him remain illiterate!" Paul seemingly anticipated that some believers would reject his teaching on miraculous works of the Spirit and added this harsh warning: "If anyone thinks himself to be a prophet or spiritual, let him acknowledge that the things which I write to you are the commandments of the Lord" (1 Cor. 14:37).

What are the commandments of which he speaks? The answer, in part, regards the apostolic teachings regarding spiritual gifts. We are no more at liberty to reject these biblically mandated instructions than any other commandment of the Lord. Until recent years there has probably been no other subject the church was more ignorant of or more eager to reject than spiritual gifts. Instead of heeding Paul's instruction, the church has engaged in deliberate, open defiance against them. This was done in full view of Paul's exhortations.

1. "Earnestly desire the best gifts" (1 Cor. 12:31).

2. "Pursue love, and desire spiritual gifts, ...especially that you may prophesy" (14:1).

3. "Since you are zealous for spiritual gifts, let it be for the edification of the church that you seek to excel" (14:12).

4. "Come short in no gift, eagerly waiting for the revelation of our Lord Jesus Christ" (1:7).

Observe the emphatic words: *Earnestly desire, pursue, zealous, seek to excel,* and *come short in no gift.* These do not indicate the apathetic attitude characteristic of today's church. Instead, Scripture explicitly encourages believers to *exercise the gifts for the benefit of everyone:*

> But the manifestation of the Spirit is given to each one for the profit of all: for to one is given the word of wisdom through the Spirit, to another the word of knowledge through the same Spirit, to another faith by the same Spirit, to another gifts of healings by the same Spirit, to another the working of miracles, to another prophecy, to another discerning of spirits, to another different kinds of tongues, to another the interpretation of tongues. But one and the same Spirit works all these things, distributing to each one individually as He wills... But if anyone is ignorant, let him be ignorant.
> —1 CORINTHIANS 12:7–14:38

Categories of Gifts

The nine charismatic endowments (see 1 Corinthians 12:4–11), may be divided into three groups, each with three gifts. Significantly, the trinity—Father, Son, and Holy Spirit—are identified in the arrangement.

1. "Diversities of gifts, but the same [Holy] Spirit" (v. 4).

2. "Differences of ministries, but the same Lord" [Jesus] (v. 5).

3. "Diversities of activities, but it is the same God" [the Father] (v. 6).

To violate these gifts or their arrangement violates the work of the Godhead. To conscientious believers in the Word of God, such a violation borders on blasphemy. Scripture divides the groupings in this way:

1. *Revelation Gifts:* word of wisdom, word of knowledge, discerning of spirits.

2. *Vocal Gifts:* tongues, interpretation, prophecy.

3. *Power Gifts:* faith, healing, working of miracles.

When the writer of Hebrews spoke of those who have "tasted the heavenly gift" and experienced the "powers of the age to come," he referred to those who minister in the miraculous gifts of the Holy Spirit (see Hebrews 6:4–5). This should excite believers. Though still living in the present world system, we are privileged to operate in the "powers of the age to come." That is a staggering realization.

Humbled by Tongues

Of all the Spirit's gifts, tongues is the most controversial. God has a reason for this: Speaking in tongues is the only gift deliberately designed to attack man's ego and pride. To the public, speaking in tongues is abnormal. It appears to denote mental incompetence, social inferiority and ignorance. The mere mention of this gift arouses man's religious intolerance. Curiously, these negative attitudes against the gift fulfill its unusual purpose:

> God has chosen the foolish things of the world to put to shame the wise, and God has chosen the weak things of the world to put to shame the things which are mighty; and the base things of the world and the things which are despised God has chosen, and the things which are not, to bring to nothing the things that are, that no flesh should glory in His presence.
>
> —1 Corinthians 1:27–29

No other gift achieves the humbling purpose of God like the gift of tongues. Speaking in tongues exposes vanity in people who at first may hate it but later love and appreciate it. Some, of course, will never yield. Gifts of wisdom, knowledge and faith do not anger people. Many would volunteer for gifts of healing or discerning of spirits while they want no part of the gift of tongues. God rejects that attitude. As the watch guard at the gate, the *charisma* of tongues stops many casual believers from stepping into the realm of miraculous power. Until a person can lovingly submit to the unusual nature of speaking in tongues, it is doubtful he will pass on to the Spirit's more appreciated works. For that reason, the gift of tongues is usually the first gift to manifest in those baptized in the Spirit. Even then, there is no guarantee that ego and pride will not return. After baptism in the Spirit, believers find that the "flesh lusts against the Spirit, and the Spirit against the flesh" (Gal. 5:17). Our warfare against pride is an ongoing, ceaseless one.

Why is praying in tongues so important? Paul explained the value of this gift when he said, "He who speaks in a tongue does not speak to men but to God, for no one understands him; however, in the spirit he speaks mysteries" (1 Cor. 14:2). The "mysteries" of which the apostle speaks are facts which cannot be known through ordinary intelligence. They are beyond human reach. Let me explain: The mind has only five sources of information. These are the physical senses of hearing, seeing, touching, tasting and smelling. All are wonderful, and we do not want to lose any of them. Even so, if a believer's spiritual life is limited to these natural senses, he is not even as well-equipped as animals. After all, the five senses in many animals are vastly superior to man's.

A polar bear can smell food at a distance of twenty-four miles. The common housefly can detect and respond to danger in $\frac{1}{200}$ of a second. Birds can see distances eight times greater than a human. Most dogs can detect odors one hundred times greater than you or I. Bats fly perfectly through narrow crevices in a pitch-black cave. Monarch butterflies migrate thousands of miles over unknown territory to a tiny, isolated spot in Mexico. God created man with lessor sensory ability to force his reliance on spiritual ability. However, man often refuses the miraculous resources in preference to his own stubborn ways. That loss can be tragic.

Unlike the human body, the regenerate human spirit is neither confined nor powerless; it has access to the "spirit of wisdom and revelation" which equips it to receive and use knowledge directly from the Holy Spirit. This special equipping is the precise function of the "word of knowledge, word of wisdom, discerning of spirits," and other gifts of the Holy Spirit. (See 1 Corinthians 12:8–10.) People who function in these gifts sometimes "know" things happening in other parts of the world and are able to pray effectively for them.

In his Roman letter, Paul dealt with our human inability to pray properly when he said, "We do not know what we should pray for as we ought, but the Spirit Himself makes intercession for us with groanings which cannot be uttered" (Rom. 8:26). "Groanings" in this context is not a reference to the gift of tongues, but it provides insight into the gift's purpose. God frequently uses the groaning experience and/or speaking in tongues to transfer information from the unknown spiritual realm into the understanding of the mind. Knowledge which is beyond the five physical senses may suddenly appear in the intellect. In this way, the gift of tongues sometimes makes "known to us the mystery of His will" (Eph. 1:9). Once a person understands God's purpose in providing this unusual gift, he will never again reject it.

There are two directions of the gift of tongues. The first is from God downward to the people. This is a public message which requires an interpretation. (See 1 Corinthians 14:27–28.) When Paul asked, "Do all speak with tongues?" he was referring to a message from God to the people that requires interpretation. The second direction of tongues is from the people upward to God. This may be prayer, praise, or "singing in the Spirit" (see 1 Corinthians 14:15). Regarding this gift, we are told to ask for the interpretation, which may or may not be given. (See 1 Corinthians 14:13.)

During my private religious struggle, I had no problem accepting the other gifts of the Spirit. They did not challenge me intellectually. This was not true of the gift of tongues. Nothing had ever attacked my logic and reason like this peculiar experience threatened to do. I disliked it, feared it and wanted nothing to do with it. God's method of dealing with my attitude was ultimately to make me weep for it, grieve over my rebellion against it and acknowledge my spiritually crippled state. The day I received that gift was a time of celebration and inexpressible joy.

Grace in Two Revelations

The New Testament interweaves the concept of *saving grace* and *gifting grace* so totally that to eliminate either would destroy the system embodying both. The structure of the grace system is perfect, indivisible. The Greek words for saving grace (*charis*) and gifting grace (*charisma*) are merely variations of the same term. The first is grace in the general sense; that is, grace that saves the sinner for heaven. The second is grace in the specific; that is, grace in the form of charismatic gifts that enables the redeemed saint to live in the realm of the miraculous. In other words, the operations of grace are plural, not singular. Grace does much more than redeem from sin. *It is a restorer of the damage wrought by sin.* This restoration is frequently accomplished through the operation of spiritual gifts. Physical or emotional healing is frequently needed by those who have been long born-again. Grace saves; *charisma* restores. Tragically, much of contemporary Christianity thinks it only needs saving grace. The loss is regrettable.

Grace-gift, as an external evidence of inward grace, is translated seventeen times in the New Testament as "spiritual gift" (KJV). Significantly, the word *grace* (charis) provides the first syllable in the Greek spelling of "spiritual gift"(charisma). By using the same root-word for spiritual gift and redemptive grace, the New Testament reveals a vital truth:

Key Point:

> Spiritual gifts cannot exist apart from grace. Grace cannot be fully revealed apart from spiritual gifts.

There is no exception to this rule. As a "pearl of great price," an inseparable *whole*, grace is an indivisible jewel;

to break it is to destroy it. In illustrating this truth, the Greek New Testament uses both words, *charisma* and *charis*, in the same sentence: "As each one has received a gift [*charisma*], minister it to one another, as good stewards of the manifold grace [*charis*] of God" (1 Pet. 4:10). In acknowledging the two grace functions as one, the apostle is explaining that whoever possesses the ministry gift is a steward of God's redemptive grace. In the biblical context, the word *steward* means "one entrusted with authority"; in this case, he is authorized with the ministry of spiritual gifts. As if to fortify the multiple function of grace, Peter uses the word *manifold*, meaning "various in character."

Each operation of grace compliments the other. There is no conflict between them. Men have created theological contention, but it is nonexistent in Scripture and in the intent of God. After Saul of Tarsus' encounter with Jesus on the Damascus road, he went into the city where Ananias laid hands on him to be "filled with the Holy Spirit" (Acts 9:1–19). In the precise order of the first apostles, Paul experienced *charis* (saving grace) and then *charisma* (gifting grace). As a "good steward of the manifold grace of God," Ananias administered spiritual gifts to Paul. That imparting came through the laying-on-of-hands and the baptism in the Holy Spirit. (See Acts 1:5,8.)

Much is preached about Paul's experience on the Damascus road; tragically little about what happened in the Damascus room. This loss is regrettable. On the Damascus road Paul was born again; that is, he received grace in the general sense. In the Damascus room, he received spiritual gifts; that is, specific grace, that ultimately presented him to the throne of Caesar and reshaped the history of mankind. Paul's invasion of the Roman world cannot be credited to the man himself. The Holy Spirit, using Paul's body as His temple, emptied pagan shrines and brought heathen philosophy to ruin. Grace, in the operation of spiritual gifts, accomplished these powerful works. The absence of such success today is the direct result of believers renouncing grace in its full operation. Many are willing to accept grace in the general experience but not in the specific. One thing is certain: God has not withdrawn any part of original grace.

In the same fashion that Paul received the Spirit's imparting from Ananias, he later bestowed the gift to young Timothy. (See 2 Timothy 1:6.) To the Roman church, he wrote, "I long to see you, that I may impart to you some spiritual gift, so that you may be established" (Rom. 1:11). Though Paul addressed the Romans as saints, he knew they still needed additional grace-gifts to be fully established. These gifts could not be communicated in the letter; Paul had to be present for the laying-on-of-hands.

The Miraculous Christian Life

Though it is not apparent in our English translations, Paul used the word *grace* five times to identify miraculous gifts in 1 Corinthians 12. The word *grace* (charis) appears ten times in the Book of Acts, giving equal emphasis to both its saving and gifting concepts. In Paul and Barnabas' ministry in Iconium, for example, "The Lord... was bearing witness to the word of His grace, granting signs and wonders to be done by their hands" (Acts 14:3). Observe, it was grace that produced signs and wonders. A major demonstration was the healing of the lame man at Lystra (see Acts 14:8-10). Paul's command was, "Stand up straight on your feet!" This display of grace was an exact parallel of the healing of a crippled man through Peter earlier at the temple gate in Jerusalem. Peter's command had been, "In the name of Jesus Christ of Nazareth, rise up and walk" (Acts 3:6). Though their words were different, the results were exactly the same.

In each case, the grace-gift of healing was operating. The day after the crippled man was healed in the temple, Peter and John were described this way: "With great power the apostles gave witness to the resurrection of the Lord Jesus. And *great grace* was upon them all" (Acts 4:33, emphasis added). Clearly, the most convincing proof of Jesus' resurrection was not the apostles' preaching. It was the sight of the lame man running and leaping in the temple. Grace, in the form of a spiritual gift, had touched him. This visible manifestation of healing grace spoke more powerfully to the people about the invisible reality of saving grace than did the apostles' preaching. Why had it happened? The Holy Spirit confirmed the word of grace by demonstrating a grace-gift. (See Luke 16:20.)

Key Point:

> It was not grace as a doctrine but grace as a *manifested power* that proved Jesus to be alive.

A similar demonstration of grace is described when Barnabas arrived in Antioch: "When he came and had *seen* the grace of God, he was glad..." (Acts 11:23, emphasis added). How did Barnabas *see* grace in action? Multitudes were born again, healed, cleansed from demons, baptized in the Spirit, and experienced other life-changing transformations. We have the same pattern when the disciples "went out and preached everywhere, the Lord working with them and confirming the word through the accompanying signs" (Mark 16:20). Two things happened: The disciples preached the word of grace, and the Holy Spirit validated its truth by bestowing grace-gifts. The presence of grace was evidenced by miraculous signs. These manifestations were visible and tangible—obvious to the eye.

46

Jewish authorities had been able to deny the apostles' preaching, but after the healing of the lame man at the temple gate, they had this to say of Peter and John: "That a notable miracle has been done through them is evident to all who dwell in Jerusalem, and we cannot deny it" (Acts 4:16). Had the disciples held to the modern concept of a disrupted grace-system, these miracles would never have taken place. Now, as then, the miraculous life should identify every Christian life.

In introducing the Book of Acts, Luke emphasized two aspects in the ministry of Jesus: "The former account I made, O Theophilus, of all that Jesus began both to do and teach" (Acts 1:1). The ministry of Jesus was *doing and teaching*. This is the pattern intended for all New Testament disciples then and now. Our teaching is to be confirmed by "signs following." Both aspects are required if grace is to be fully revealed through us.

The perfect structure of New Testament grace has a parallel in the structure of Old Testament law. Like grace, the law was an indivisible whole. No one could add to it; no one could take from it. To violate one point made the offender guilty of the law's total consequence. Christians have no difficulty accepting this Old Testament truth. At the identical point of comparison, many refuse to make the same application to the New Testament's grace-system. Bias against spiritual gifts is so deeply ingrained that some claiming to believe in the inerrancy of Scripture will argue that 1 Corinthians 11 is valid, but twelve is not. Thirteen is valid, but fourteen is not, and so on. Such hopscotch theology emasculates the Word of God.

Key Point:

> Believing in grace and in grace-gifts is one and the same belief. Denying grace and grace-gifts is one and the same denial.

If we accept Paul's statement to the Ephesians, "For by grace [charis] you have been saved through faith" (Eph. 2:8), we are equally obligated to accept his statement to the Corinthians regarding gifts of healings (charismata) by the same Spirit. (See 1 Corinthians 12:9.) The expression, "by the same Spirit" gives unchallengeable authority to the reality of grace-gifts. To deny them is to disrupt the operation of grace as an inviolate, God-designed pattern. We are commanded to preach the full system of grace. Redemptive grace without gifting grace is an abortion of truth; it is a contradiction of terms. Without hesitation we must preach that "man shall not live by bread alone, but by *every word* of God" (Luke 4:4, emphasis added). That includes *all* New Testament teachings about the full operation of grace. Grace cannot be divided; it must be accepted as an indivisible unit. Scripture solemnly warns us against abusing grace. Three forms of abuse are to:

1. "receive the grace of God in vain" (2 Cor. 6:1).

2. "set aside the grace of God" (Gal. 2:21).

3. "insult the Spirit of grace" (see Hebrews 10:29).

Opposition to the grace-system does not originate within the church; it comes from powers of darkness projecting itself upon the church. Satan does not fear man. He fears the Spirit's grace-gifts operating in man and will go to any length to stop them. Remember that Satan appeared to Jesus immediately after His anointing in the Jordan River. Today, the devil tries to stop us *before* we receive the Holy Spirit's power. If he can prevent that through unbelief, fear or harassment, he will. In cases where individuals have already received the imparting, he erects barricades to handicap them. This attack should not intimidate the Spirit-filled believer who knows that "He who is in you is greater than he who is in the world" (1 John 4:4).

The Gift of the Spirit Imparted

We have many good examples from Scripture of how the Holy Spirit was imparted. Let's look at those and then see how they apply to us today.

1. "He breathed on them and said to them, 'Receive the Holy Spirit'" (John 20:22).

2. "Tarry in... Jerusalem until you are endued with power from on high" (Luke 24:49).

3. "They were all filled with the Holy Spirit" (Acts 2:4).

4. "Stephen, full of faith and power, did great wonders and signs..." (Acts 6:8).

5. "They laid hands on them, and they received the Holy Spirit" (Acts 8:17).

6. Ananias said to Saul: "...that you may be... filled with the Holy Spirit" (Acts 9:17).

7. "The Holy Spirit fell upon all those who heard the word" (Acts 10:44).

8. "Did you receive the Holy Spirit when you believed?" (Acts 19:2).

10. "The manifestation of the Spirit is given to each one for the profit of all" (1 Cor. 12:7).

49

Now let's see how the Lord can enable you to experience His miraculous gifts in your own life and ministry.

1. First of all, He desires to *normalize* our lives. (See Luke 8:35.)

2. Next, He wants to *empower* our lives. (See Acts 1:8.)

3. Ultimately, He will *glorify* our lives. (See John 17:10, 22.)

Lives that are empowered without being normalized are dangerous; lives that are normalized without being glorified are incomplete. The ultimate work of grace is total, absolute and final. God desires that we be normalized, empowered and glorified.

The Spirit Chooses the Ministry

Each ministry of the Spirit must be directed specifically by Him. Only then can the anointing operate in its own power. Human understanding is vastly inadequate for such a task. The apostle John explains, "You have an anointing [*chrisma*] from the Holy One, and you know all things" (1 John 2:20). This expression, "know all things" refers to believers being instructed by the Holy Spirit to minister as the Father directs. Consequently, we are not to "lay hands on anyone hastily" (1 Tim. 5:22). We are not at liberty to follow our own choices. Jesus Himself acknowledged, "The Son can do nothing of Himself, but what He sees the Father do; for whatever He does, the Son also does in like manner" (John 5:19). Additionally, He explained, "My doctrine is not Mine but His who sent me" (John 7:16).

Our major problem is we do not wait to hear what "the Spirit says to the churches" but rush ahead, mistakenly thinking our enthusiasm is faith. (See Revelation 2:11.) In that urgency, we miss instruction from the "still small voice" (1 Kings 19:12). God does not fail. Nor does He want us to fail. When failure happens, it is because we did not listen and obey. Jesus said, "My sheep hear My voice" (John 10:27).

As a pastor in Atlanta, I once received a phone call from parents in Augusta, Georgia, whose daughter had run away from home. They had no idea where she was but thought she might have come to Atlanta. So I prayed, asking the Lord for a word of knowledge.

At that time, Atlanta had a population of nearly two million, and my finding the girl accidentally was impossible. Almost instantly the Holy Spirit impressed my mind with the name of a local bar which I recalled by its blatant advertising. Without moving from the chair, I called the lounge and asked if they would put a note on their bulletin board. It began with the girl's name; it simply said, "You don't have to come home, but please call" and closed with the parents' names. That was all.

Two weeks later the family visited our Sunday service. They told how after I called the bar, the girl came in and saw the note from her parents. She was shocked into the realization that it was God who was pursuing her, not merely her mom and dad. That fact broke through her rebellion and sent her home. Grace, as a specific word of knowledge, had touched her life.

Another time a young woman, vivacious and happy, visited our church office and chatted light-heartedly. Her grandfather was one of the most appreciated clergymen in our community. As we prayed, the Holy Spirit said, "Take command over the spirit of suicide."

I was startled by the clarity of the message. The girl seemed too cheerful and happy to be dealing with that problem. But the same instruction came again. This time I obeyed, looked at her, and in a quiet, authoritative voice, commanded the spirit of suicide to go.

She stared at me incredulously, "How did you know?" she asked, pulling up her long sleeves to reveal ugly scars where she had already slashed her wrists.

"The Holy Spirit told me," I explained. "He loves you and will set you free." And He did.

On another occasion a young Jamaican woman with multiple sclerosis and vision of 20/75, came forward for ministry. She was healed of the sclerosis and her eyesight became 20/25.

An older woman, suffering from severe shingles and confined to home asked for prayer. The doctors had warned she would be months in recovery. I anointed her with oil, prayed and left. There was nothing significant about our time together. At five o'clock the next morning, she got out of bed, and as she removed her gown, the scales fell off. She was healed.

A young male African-American in California who had suffered a serious back injury had not worked in two years and been under the care of eight doctors. He was healed in a five-minute ministry of laying on of hands and prayer.

A young woman in Tennessee who had been injured in a horseback riding accident and depended on crutches was told by physicians that she would never recover. In a few minutes of prayer she was totally healed and left the meeting walking normally. Her mother carried the crutches out of the building, waving them over her head.

These examples are only a sampling to show the variety of ways the Holy Spirit demonstrates His power. I can never again become an unbeliever. I have seen too many instances of the Holy Spirit using grace-gifts to bless saints and sinners alike. Ordinary people with extraordinary problems can fall into the embrace of a super-ordinary Jesus. He is the avenue through whom all grace, general and specific, touches mankind.

Chapter Four

You Can Minister in the Power of the Holy Spirit

As an earnest believer, you are an heir of this promise: "In My name... they will lay hands on the sick, and they will recover" (Mark 16:17–18). Jesus was speaking to you when He said this. Do not be afraid to trust it, and be certain that you do not become trapped in other people's unbelief. Well-meaning people will destroy your faith if you let them. For years I was a victim of Christianized skepticism that bore deadly fruit in my life. Disguised as truth, and sounding like truth, it is Satan's most effective destroyer of faith.

Laying on of Hands

The young man who wrote the following letter tells how he was healed through the laying-on-of-hands:

Dear Brother Charles... I fell ten feet off a roof and landed with all my weight on my left leg. The impact completely shattered my ankle, tore my skin, and broke the fibula just below my knee. They took me to surgery and literally wired and screwed my leg back together... The doctor said he had no idea how long I would have to wear the fixiter around my ankle. But he said when he took it off, he would put my leg in a cast... The month before your visit, the X-rays still showed much separation in my ankle. My skin had just started fusing together, but the fibula was still in two separate pieces. During your visit, you laid hands on me and prayed three times for my leg.

The Monday you left, the doctor took more X-rays. He came into my room and examined my leg. Then he looked at my X-rays. He got a very puzzled look on his face. He turned and examined my leg again. I looked over his shoulder at the X-rays. All the ankle pieces were in place. The skin showed no sign of being broken, and the fibula was whole. With the same funny look on his face he looked at the X-rays again. Then he walked out of the room.

When he came back he seemed confused. He examined the X-rays again, then moved to my side. He placed his left hand under my heel and his right hand on top of my shin. As he pushed down on the shin he pulled up on my heel. He told me to tell him if I felt any pain. There was none. That funny look was on his face again. He then placed his right hand on the inside of my calf, placed his left on the outside of my foot. As he pushed and pulled, he again told me to say if felt any pain. There was none. He did the same thing in the opposite direction. Again, no pain. The force he was using caused his arms to shake; he was using every bit of force he could. He looked at my leg and the X-rays again and again.

Finally, he threw his hands up and said, "I'm taking it off." Then he told me there was no need for a cast... I can now walk for short periods without my crutches. The only discomfort is from exercising the muscles and tendons which have been immobile for four months... I am at least three months ahead of my doctor's expected progress of healing and he can't explain why. Isn't God great?!"

—KEN NOWELL
FLORENCE, ALABAMA

How does the Holy Spirit use one person to heal another? Let me explain: When a ministering-temple rightly lays hands on a receiving-temple, as in this young man's case, there is movement of the Holy Spirit from the first to the second. Sometimes this can be felt physically. Electric current arching from one terminal to another illustrates this transfer of power. The person may experience some indication that they have been touched by the power of God. In the case of this young man, however, I can recall nothing visible taking place at the time I laid hands on him.

Some ask: Isn't there a danger of people experiencing a purely emotional response when someone lays hands on them, or even their faking such an experience? The answer is yes. For that reason, the one ministering must do everything in his power to guard against such an attitude. But we must also remember this: baptism, communion, worship, all other Christian exercises can be counterfeited by those willing to do so. We need to realize, too, that Satan would not fake something unless he has reason to fear its authentic counterpart.

References to laying-on-of-hands appear some twenty-eight times in the New Testament. Only four or five times does it refer to the ordination of pastors, elders, deacons, etc. All other instances regard healing, ministering the baptism in the Spirit and the imparting of other spiritual

55

gifts. The significance of this ministry is most clearly demonstrated in the scriptural teaching that our bodies are the "temple of the Holy Spirit" (1 Cor. 6:19). Please understand this carefully: It is the temple of the Holy Spirit inside your body through which the power is released. The human hand by itself is powerless.

Gifts Work as God Wills

God wills that miraculous "signs" occur in your ministry. When that grace-power appears, amazing things will happen, and you and those to whom you minister will be blessed. Expect it!

Wonderfully, you may find all or some of these gifts working in you:

1. word of wisdom—Luke 24:45; Genesis 41:33–40
2. word of knowledge—John 4:17–18; 1 Samuel 10:2–13
3. gift of faith—Mark 5:34; Daniel 3:16–17
4. gifts of healings—Luke 4:39; 11 Kings 5:10
5. working of miracles—Acts 19:36–43; Genesis 18:14
6. gift of prophecy—Acts 21:8–11; 1 Samuel 10:10
7. discerning of spirits—Acts 16:16–18; 1 Kings 22:20–22
8. gift of tongues—Acts 19:6; Isaiah 28:9–12
9. tongues with interpretation—Acts 2:6; Zephaniah 3:9

You cannot force these gifts to operate. As God wills, they will work through you. The gift of tongues is the one exception that operates at your discretion. You can, and should, pray frequently "in the Spirit." While many people will rejoice at the miraculous works taking place in you, others may not. Be forewarned but do not be discouraged when this happens. People are sometimes fearful of what they do not understand, and the visible operation of the Spirit's gifts alarms them. Paul explained, "The natural man does not receive the things of the Spirit of God, for

You Can Minister in the Power of the Holy Spirit

they are foolishness to him; nor can he know them, because they are spiritually discerned" (1 Cor. 2:14). It should not surprise us, therefore, that Pentecost, in ancient times or present times, is startling to people. Observe how Scripture describes this when the Holy Spirit came on the disciples who were waiting in Jerusalem:

"And there were dwelling in Jerusalem Jews, devout men, from every nation under heaven. And when this sound occurred [Pentecost], the multitude came together" (Acts 2:5–6). The people responded in the following ways:

1. They "were confused" (2:6).
2. "They were all amazed" (2:7).
3. "They were all amazed and perplexed" (2:12).
4. "Others mocking said, 'They are full of new wine'" (2:13).

It was not the irreligious people who suffered confusion, amazement and perplexity on the Day of Pentecost; it was the devout people. Many sincere Christians experience the same difficulty with the unusual manifestations of the Holy Spirit as did first-century Jews. It is unrealistic for us to assume that all godly people will automatically recognize a genuine move of the Spirit. They will not.

The accusation that believers on the day of Pentecost were drunk is no different from accusations today. Many who experience the Holy Spirit's miraculous power are unable to control its effects. While the New Testament does not identify the specific "signs and wonders" that occurred, we do know that on the day of Pentecost believers were in a drunken-like condition—their physical bodies overcome by the presence of God. When overwhelmed by that presence, people may collapse to the floor, jerk, groan, vibrate or laugh uncontrollably. Why does that happen? Simply explained, the human body cannot cope with the surge of spiritual power. I have seen

57

sophisticated priests, pastors and very self-disciplined preachers be seized with body-shaking power. In the early years of the Quaker movement in England, the people were often overcome with bodily shaking. The name *Quakers* originated from this unusual manifestation.

Our physical bodies' inability to endure such power surge should not surprise us. Ezekiel, Jeremiah, Daniel, Abraham, Saul of Tarsus and numerous others fell to the earth when confronted by God's presence. While you must not be afraid of these manifestations, it is important to understand that jerking, shaking and falling is not what the Spirit is trying to accomplish. These are merely the side effects of His presence. Whether a person shakes, laughs, stands or falls is not a test of the Spirit's work. Changed lives, bodies and minds are the proof we seek.

When Pentecost caused alarm in the people, Peter counteracted it this way:

1. He defended Pentecost scripturally: "This is what was spoken by the prophet Joel" (Acts 2:16).

2. He vindicated Pentecost's miracles, wonders, and signs by relating them to the ministry of Jesus. (See Acts 2:22.)

3. Peter related himself to the people: "Listen carefully, all of you, fellow Jews and residents of Jerusalem!" (Acts 2:14, NLT).

4. He affirmed that Pentecost was proof of Jesus' resurrection. He and other disciples were witnesses. (See Acts 2:32.) Jesus had been glorified. (See John 7:39.)

5. He called the people to their own accountability in the crucifixion. (See Acts 2:36.)

6. Peter offered repentance, baptism and the remission of sins as the opportunity for the people to receive the promised gift of the Holy Spirit. (See Acts 2:38–39.)

After hearing the apostle's message, whose who had been previously confused "were cut to the heart, and said to Peter and the rest of the apostles, 'Men and brethren, what shall we do?' Then Peter said to them, "Repent... and you shall receive the gift of the Holy Spirit" ...That day about three thousand souls were added to them" (Acts 2:37–38, 41). Those who only moments before were resistant and confused about Pentecost quickly accepted it.

When you minister to those caught in the web of confusion, you must remember to be patient and gracious to them.

> A servant of the Lord must not quarrel but be gentle to all, able to teach, patient, in humility correcting those who are in opposition, if God perhaps will grant them repentance, so that they may know the truth, and that they may come to their senses and escape the snare of the devil, having been taken captive by him to do his will (2 Tim. 2:24–26).

In one of my meetings, a father and son came forward for prayer for the boy's failing eyesight. Serious problems potentially threatened him. When I laid hands on both of them, the father instantly slammed to the floor while the youth stood there, seemingly unaffected; for a moment he waited, envying his father's experience. He expected an outward sign and felt rejected when it did not happen. Even so, the wonderful fact that he was also touched was soon confirmed by his doctor: He was healed.

In Samaria, Peter laid hands on the people. (See Acts 8:17.) In Caesarea he did not. (See Acts 10:44.) In both cases, the results were explosively the same: Peter's temple was present. In Caesarea the power fell without his physical contact. The same principle was true when Peter walked the streets of Jerusalem, and invalids were healed by the touch of his shadow. (See Acts 5:15.) There is no healing power in a shadow. Rather, it was the nearness of Peter's temple-body and the anointing radiating from it that brought miraculous results. This factor explains how aprons and handkerchiefs as extensions of Paul's body carried healing power. (See Acts 19:12.)

Those who minister in the anointing sometimes feel the power leaving their temple but failing to enter the other party. Several factors may cause this. There may be unrecognized resistance in the one receiving ministry. That impregnability may come from pride, fear, jealousy, unforgiveness, an undesirable spirit or a variety of other influences. Your faith as well as the one receiving is essential. Faith is expectation. The authority of the Word must assume greater influence than the opposition. Divine truth as revealed in Scripture must be incontestable fact: "He who is in you is greater than he who is in the world" (1 John 4:4).

Key Point:

Apart from the indwelling of the Holy Spirit, the human hand has no merit whatever.

Through the power of the Holy Spirit, many spiritual gifts have been imparted through the laying on of hands. Here are some biblical examples.

1. Imparted by Moses: "Take Joshua... a man in whom is the Spirit, and lay your hand on him" (Num. 27:18).

2. Received by Joshua: "Joshua... was full of the spirit of *wisdom*, for Moses had laid his hands on him" (Deut. 34:9, italics added).

3. Imparted by believers: "They will lay hands on the sick, and they will recover" (Mark 16:18).

4. Received by Paul: "Laying his hands on him [Ananias], said, 'Brother Saul... receive your sight and be filled with the Holy Spirit" (Acts 9:17).

5. Imparted by Paul: "Laying on of the hands of the eldership" (1 Tim. 4:14).

6. Received by Timothy: "In you through the laying on of my hands" (2 Tim. 1:6).

7. Imparted by the apostles: "Signs and wonders to be done by their hands" (Acts 14:3).

8. Received by the people in Iconium: "A great multitude both of the Jews and of the Greeks believed" (Acts 14:1).

9. Imparted by Jesus: "When He had spit on his eyes... and put His hands on him" (Mark 8:23).

10. Received by the blind man: "Then He put His hands on his eyes again and made him look up. And he was restored and saw everyone clearly" (Mark 8:25).

11. Imparted by Paul; received by the Romans: "I long to see you, that I may impart to you some spiritual gift, so that you may be established" (Rom. 1:11).

Laying-On-of-Hands in Baptist History

Welsh Tract Baptist Church, located in northern Delaware, was constituted in South Wales about 1702 for the specific purpose of migrating to North America. Their government included a pastor, elder, deacon, teaching elder and ruling elder. With four other American churches, they formed the first Baptist association of Philadelphia and adopted the 1689 London Confession of Faith as their statement of belief. In 1742, they added two articles to the confession: 1) the singing of psalms; and

2) laying-on-of-hands. These two points were important in Welsh Baptist theology, and they insisted they become part of the confession. As historic Baptists they believed that the "Holy Spirit of Promise" was imparted through the laying-on-of-hands. (See Acts 1:4–5; Ephesians 1:13–14.) American church history would be very different today had Baptists maintained this scriptural practice.

Before laying hands on anyone, remember the scriptural injunction, "Do not lay hands on anyone hastily" (1 Tim. 5:22). You must have the Holy Spirit's specific instruction for each ministry. That knowledge can come in a flash; oftentimes I will have the Spirit's immediate "release" to minister to everyone in a long, long line. Other times He will stop me.

When you are ready to proceed, be certain the people understand the scriptural basis for what is happening. Explain that they must:

1. Be repentant, submitted to the Lord.
2. Consciously surrender all self-control.
3. Forgive others totally and unconditionally.
4. Break all association with the occult.
5. Release their faith, open up and drop resistance.
6. Receive. Take in. Spiritually inhale. Jesus said, "Drink."

Prayer is outgoing; this is a time of incoming. If necessary, have them pause in their praying and *receive*. Jesus said, "Drink." People will sometimes pray feverishly during hands-on ministry as if their effort will make God move in their behalf. The idea is wrong. Have them stop and drink!

Falling Under the Spirit's Power

Jonathan Edwards, whose preaching ignited Colonial America's Great Awakening, was well-acquainted with the experience of people falling under the power of the Holy Spirit. He wrote, "If there be a very powerful influence of the Spirit of God in a mixed multitude, it will cause in some way or other a great visible commotion."[1] During his 1740 ministry, his wife, Sarah, fell under the power of the Spirit. According to her diary, she "swooned" and remained "without bodily strength" for *seventeen* days. Later, she said of that remarkable experience:

> I was aware of the delightful sense of the presence of the Lord, and I became conscious of His *nearness* to me—and my *dearness* to Him.[2]

At one point Sarah determined that she had to resume her household duties, and, rising from bed, passed the room where her husband and another man were talking. When she heard the name "Jesus," she was immediately slammed to the floor. The two men carried her up the stairs and placed her in bed. Only when the Spirit's presence lifted could she return to work. Why did it happen? What was God's purpose for Sarah's seventeen-day communion with the Holy Spirit? Obviously, we cannot know heaven's reason, but ponder this thought: All great moves of the Spirit are initiated and maintained through prayer. It may be that Sarah's seventeen-day seclusion was God's method of providing needed intercession to carry the Great Awakening to its climax. One thing we know: God had an urgent purpose which was best accomplished by Sarah's complete isolation with Him. Before the Great Awakening began, her husband, Jonathan, prayed for twelve hours in an empty baptistery. That intercession opened the gates of heaven for the Holy Spirit to fall upon New England. All men and women who have been greatly used of God and through whom "signs and wonders" appeared were men and women of travailing prayer.

George Whitefield and John Wesley are examples of such men. In the beginning, Whitefield did not understand the "sign" of people falling in Wesley's ministry and rebuked him for it. Not long afterward it happened in George's preaching. By the time he came to Boston in the mid-1700's, he was wise enough to command people in the trees to come down. He knew that once the power of the Holy Spirit fell upon the congregation, many of them would drop to the ground like stones.

At the famous 1801 Cane Ridge, Kentucky, camp meeting, over five hundred were felled at one time. Many were knocked from their horses.[3] Pastor James Glindening, a Puritan of sixteenth-century England, had the deacons remove the fallen from his congregation and lay them under the trees. Peter Cartwright, Charles Fenny, and hosts of other historic preachers witnessed it in their meetings.[4] It even happened in Baptist meetings in early America—as it has happened throughout the history of Christianity. When it happens, don't let it scare you. It is God.

Natural vs. Spiritual Falling

The Scripture provides important insight between falling in the natural and spiritual aspects. Variations in the Greek spelling are slight but important. Observe this:

1. "Peter went up on the housetop to pray, about the sixth hour. Then he became very hungry and wanted to eat; but while they made ready, he *fell* into a trance" (Acts 10:9–10, italics added). Peter's falling experience was spiritual. "Fell" is the Greek word *epipipto*.

2. "As Peter was coming in, Cornelius... *fell* down at his feet and worshiped him" (Acts 10:25). Here, referring to a purely physical experience, "fell" is translated from *pipto*.

3. "While Peter was still speaking these words, the Holy

Spirit *fell* upon all those who heard the word" (Acts 10:44). As in the first reference, the Holy Spirit's falling was spiritual. Here, Scripture returns to *epipipto*.

The same word, *epipipto*, is used when the father of the prodigal son falls on the boy's neck and hugs him. (See Luke 15:20.) It is used again of Eutychus, the young man who was killed in his fall from the "third story" whom the apostle Paul "fell on" in affection and restored to life. (See Acts 20:10.) In every instance in the New Testament *epipipto* carries an emotional or spiritual implication. When godly fear "fell" upon Zacharias, that intense emotion was present (see Luke 1:12). When "falling" is used in the spiritual sense and holy passion is expressed, it means "to be embraced with affection."

Key Point:

Those who fall under the power of the Holy Spirit are being embraced with God's affection.

What happened to Sarah Edwards and others like her was very real and very wonderful. Sarah did not fake this intimacy with the Holy Spirit any more than the numerous Old Testament saints who fell before the Lord. (See Ezekiel 1:28; 3:23; Daniel 8:17.) The Roman soldiers who approached Jesus in Gethsemane, "drew back and fell to the ground" (John 18:6). Many whom I have observed in this state are healed, delivered from unclean spirits, filled with the Holy Spirit, and "embraced" in other wonderful ways.

Practical Experiences With Falling Under the Spirit's Power

Understandably, the sight of hundreds of people dropping to the church floor is alarming to those unprepared for it.

To avoid fear in the congregation, it is important to have catchers behind each person undergoing ministry. This will remove anxiety in the audience and encourage less-courageous souls to step forward for prayer. It is also possible that some misguided person may purposely fall. This is unwise and unsafe. Avoid that danger.

The gentleman who wrote the following letter, a Southern Baptist and unaccustomed to the falling experience, had this to say after a dramatic encounter with the Holy Spirit:

> Dear Brother Carrin, I was using a table saw and almost amputated my four fingers. The doctor performed surgery to reattach the nerves and tendons. I have been in pain with my fingers and wrist ever since. When my wife and I went to your meeting the Holy Spirit touched me in a way I had never known before. When you laid hands on me, I fell under the power of the Spirit. The next evening, while doing my therapy, the bones in my wrist began to pop, and the pain immediately went away. God heals and answers prayer! Sincerely,
>
> —RALPH COGGINS
> LITHONIA, GEORGIA.

On another occasion, an atheist college professor and Ph.D. who had devoted his career to philosophy—particularly the teachings of Carl Marx—attended a meeting where I spoke. During the time I was praying and laying-on hands, I went to him. "As a philosopher," I said, "you are one who loves wisdom and want to know the truth."

"Yes," he answered. "That is true."

"If God is real," I went on, "you want to know that."

He answered hesitantly, "Yes, *if* God is real, I want to know it."

"Are you willing to say, 'God, if You are real, show me?'"

"Yes," he answered self-confidently. "I can say that."

With my encouragement, he repeated the prayer. I left him briefly, prayed with a few others, and came back. When I returned, I never spoke, but lightly touched him on his cheek. The brush of my finger knocked him to the floor. Nor did he fall gently; he went down with a jolt, grabbing at the air. For some twenty minutes he lay immobile, weeping. When he finally came up, he was still weeping, saying, "I found God! I found God!"

The pastor of a large liturgical church in the city where I served became concerned because his members were attending our services, getting delivered, filled with the Holy Spirit, and discovering the power of God. When he learned about their "falling under the power," he announced that he too would attend and prove the experience to be fake. The night he came, he wore no clerical collar; I did not know who he was. At the end of the message when I began praying for the people, he sprang to his feet and strode down the aisle. The back of the building was filled with his members anxiously watching. As he hurried toward me, I reached out my hand, but before I touched him, he was slammed to the floor. God has His own way of dealing with Christianized unbelievers. Later, I said to his members: "My warning to skeptics is: 'Don't dare God!'"

In Delray Beach, Florida, a young professional basketball player from Norway was saved, and we immediately took him to the ocean for baptism. The water was calm, clear as glass, and every sandy ripple visible on the bottom. After my assistant and I immersed and raised him up, I explained that I would lay hands on him to be filled with the Holy Spirit. His response was, "I want everything God has for me!" He was totally yielded. The instant I touched his forehead, he hit the water with a splash, body vibrating electrically, and chattering in tongues. He was semi-conscious, embraced with God's affection in a spectacular way. I quickly placed my shoulder under his head and supported him. I had never seen anyone more suspended in the glory of God, quaking in the presence of the Holy Spirit.

For a few minutes I held him up, then backed away and let him sink. As the other pastor and I watched, he went straight to the bottom. A moment later, he floated to the top, and as his face broke through the surface, he continued praying ecstatically in tongues. This happened a number of times. Half an hour later, we carried him across the beach and put him in the car. Even in the ocean, that young man discovered what it was like to be "embraced by the Holy Spirit."

The Test of New Testament Preaching

- A powerless, inefficient ministry is an insult to the Holy Spirit.
- A dysfunctional church is a humiliation to the Holy Spirit.
- A dying denomination is denial of the Holy Spirit.

The Holy Spirit still anoints the Scripture that He inspired to be written. Whoever preaches the truth of the Word can expect the Holy Spirit's anointing to accompany the Word. Churches who argue as to which has correct doctrine can answer their question by this simple test: Who is getting authentic New Testament results? It is impossible to preach New Testament truth in the anointing of the Holy Spirit and not get New Testament results. The apostle Paul settled this argument for the Corinthians by saying, "I will come..., and I will know, not the word of those who are puffed up, but the power" (1 Cor. 4:19–20). He forewarned his opponents that they would have to prove the validity of their teaching by presenting the Holy Spirit's action. The test still works.

In preaching, if the Holy Spirit is not moving in power and demonstration, then something is wrong with that specific ministry. The most common causes of failure are pride, unbelief and condemnation. The first two are more easily detected than the last; they are more obvious. Condemnation, however, can easily come upon a man or woman who is not affected by pride or unbelief. Self-disapproval, the sense of personal failure, warps a ministry by smothering it in unworthiness and guilt. Its end result is as deadly to successful ministry as flagrant sin.

Hopefully, every Christian speaker is motivated by true godliness and purity of heart. Even so, none of us are ever sufficiently worthy to merit the anointing. God's motivation in giving the anointing is His grace. But hear me carefully: Humility of heart and reverence for God are companions with which the anointing feels compatible. It finds no hindrance in working with and through them.

Chapter Five

Jesus Has an Engagement Ring for You

On a flight out of West Palm Beach, Florida, we had just become airborne over the ocean when a boy sitting next to the window grabbed my arm. "Look out there!" he said urgently. "Look!" What I saw was one of the most magnificent sights of my life. Reaching down to the surface of the ocean and rising overhead as far as I could see was the full, unbroken circle of a rainbow. The color was indescribably brilliant with the lower part of the ring seeming to float on the surface of the water. There was no gap in it—just the breathtaking color of God's beautiful sign of covenant. (See Genesis 9:13.)

I had learned a short time before that the complete rainbow, like the wedding band, is a continuous ring. It is much, much more than the mere half circle we see from ground level. At best, our earth-bound view reveals only part. To behold the bow's full circumference it is necessary to be above the earth looking down. The spiritual application of that truth is obvious: In this present life, we grasp only a fragment of the wisdom and strategy of God. Not until we are in heaven looking back at history will we be able to understand the full scope of His plan and purpose in our lives. But there on the plane, in an astonishing way, I realized the rainbow message also involves the operation of spiritual gifts. When you, too, grasp this holy truth, seeing yourself wearing an engagement ring from Christ, already seated with Him "in the heavenly places," it will release faith powerfully within you. (See Ephesians 1:3, 20.)

This truth is seldom seen but will be absolutely magnificent once you grasp it. The foundation is laid in the story of Isaac's bride. Abraham sent his servant to get a bride for his son Isaac. The young woman chosen for this honor was Rebekah. In scriptural typology, Abraham represents God the Father; the unnamed servant represents the Holy Spirit; Isaac represents Jesus the Son. Rebekah symbolizes the bride of Christ—the church. Rebekah's name means "circles" or "loops of a rope." The imagery of the rope suggests her being "inside the circle" of God's providence and grace. This is a true concept of covenant. And in keeping with the covenant tradition, as soon as the servant identified Rebekah as God's chosen one, he presented her with golden "rings" (Gen. 24:22). The shape of these gifts—circles—conveyed an important message which Rebekah understood. They were the rope loops that encircled her engagement to Isaac.

> So it was, when the camels had finished drinking, that the man took a golden nose ring weighing half a shekel, and two bracelets for her wrists weighing ten shekels of gold (Gen. 24:22).

It is important you understand this: These bracelets and rings were not wedding gifts. They were engagement gifts. Even today, brides frequently receive two rings: one before the wedding, the other at the wedding. So it was with Rebekah. First came the engagement gifts; these were followed with wedding gifts.

In a similar way, Jesus is now offering you engagement gifts; you are part of His bride. These gifts, brought to you by the Servant, the Holy Spirit, parallel the rings Rebekah received and those given to brides today. They are the "guarantee of our inheritance until the redemption of the purchased possession" (Eph. 1:14). Your heavenly wedding gifts, which are beyond human comprehension, will not be given to you until the Marriage Supper of the Lamb. (See Revelation 19:9.) But please consider carefully the gifts which come in advance of the wedding: The charismatic gifts that the church is now receiving, by which she "tastes the powers of the age to come" are engagement gifts. (See Acts 1:5,8; Hebrews 6:5; Ephesians 1:21.) Through them, the Groom is showing His bride the "glories of His Father's house."

This parallel of Rebekah and the church is exact. While Rebekah's gifts spoke of Isaac's love, they also revealed Abraham's great wealth. Just as Rebekah had never met the man to whom she was engaged, so the church has yet to meet her royal Bridegroom.

Key Point:

> The gifts Jesus is now sending through the Holy Spirit correspond to the rings and bracelets given Rebekah by Abraham's servant.

I have spoken to numerous churches where members were still opposed to spiritual gifts. They did not understand the miraculous operations of God and drew back from them. I explained that Christians who reject the gifts of the Spirit are actually telling the Heavenly Servant,

"I don't like that bracelet. Put it back in your box! I won't wear it." Rebekah's acting in such ugliness is unthinkable. Not so with modern, self-centered Christians. Many become irate, incensed, at the mere suggestion of their experiencing the Holy Spirit's miraculous gifts. The gift of tongues is the primary offender because it is the only grace-gift deliberately designed to attack ego and pride. Thankfully, many in these congregations have seen the ugliness of rejecting spiritual gifts and have come forward, repentant, saying, "I don't fully understand the Holy Spirit's gifting, but I want whatever bracelet God has for me! Pray that I will receive it!"

The View From Above

There will be times when ministry is discouraging, life seems unfair, disappointing, painful, and you will need reminding that the view from above is very different from the one below. In those moments, you will benefit tremendously from the assurance divine gifts bring to your life.

After God miraculously rescued him from a failed suicide attempt nearly three centuries ago, William Cowper wrote a hymn that has since blessed millions. In that famous lyric, "God Moves in a Mysterious Way His Wonders to Perform," Cowper said,

> "Cheer up, ye saints, fresh courage take,
> The clouds you so much dread
> Are rich with mercies and shall break
> In blessings on your head...

—PUBLIC DOMAIN

The words of Cowper's song and the incredible beauty of God's covenant-sign were still going through my mind as our plane left the rainbow behind. Leaning back in a state of awe, a series of revelations began flooding me. First was

74

the amazing, spiritual beauty of the bow; its colors were ethereal, unreal. Second, its endless circle, representing the complete cycle of God's loving, sovereign perfection in creation, was overwhelming. Nothing was omitted from its meaning. The smallest, microscopic sea life in the ocean below me to the largest galaxy in space were all contained in the scope of His unified plan. What I glimpsed in that fleeting moment was the glory of the kingdom of God. Wonderfully, the apex of that revelation was heaven's grace to man, who was destined to rule and reign in that ever-expanding, unending kingdom. For a moment, I was overwhelmed with the two-fold manifestation of grace:

1. Through saving-grace, man is prepared for divine life in heaven.
2. Through gifting-grace, man is prepared for miraculous life on earth.

In that flashing moment I understood more about the grace of God than ever before. This fact seized me: *God intended that the ordinary Christian life be a miraculous life.* Once grace touches us, we are transformed both for eternity and for now. My mind was overwhelmed with what seemed to be giant ripples of scientific and theological fact, coming toward me from every direction. Each ripple brought a unique message about God's covenant plan. This I suddenly knew: All truth, regardless of its rising from the Old Testament or the New, whether it comes from Scripture or true scientific discovery, points toward ultimate reality: *God is one; God is love; God is power.* Creation pulsates with that oneness. Jesus is the One by whom the "worlds were framed" (Heb. 11:3, John 1:1), and is the incarnation of all three. His resurrection, as an explosion of that truth, defeated every opposing principle of disunity, hatefulness and weakness in existence.

Wonderfully, the Holy Spirit showed me the relationship between the rainbow and another biblical, covenant sign: *circumcision*. It, too, is circular. The revelation that took place that day went light years beyond everything I had understood about circumcision before. Circumcision means "circular cutting." Beginning with Abraham, every Hebrew male bore in his body this physical sign of God's covenant. Suddenly I realized that the miles-wide rainbow and the few inches of circumcision were identical. Each contained all the glory, beauty, majesty of the other.

With that realization came an important question: "Why did God place the covenant sign on the male genitals?" The answer was awesome: God willed that the conception of every Hebrew child take place in the presence of his *father's* covenant-sign. Not only so, but the father's genes for every future generation passed through his covenant ring. The creative act of conception, in which those made "in His image" and "in His likeness" (Gen. 1:26), takes place within the "circle of the covenant" (Acts 2:39).

By a painful cutting away and shedding of blood, circumcision is the uncovering of maleness. In scriptural typology, it is the exposing of man to His God. If you study the covering and uncovering of tabernacle furnishings in the Old Testament, all of which came under covenant instruction, you will understand more of the parabolic teaching present here. (See Exodus 35:12, ff.) When miraculous gifts of the Holy Spirit begin operating in us it is evidence that we have experienced additional uncovering; that is, we have removed more of the insulation separating us and God. Grace, in an ongoing, deepening revelation, is taking place.

On the plane, my understanding about the covenant sign (that is, the circle) continued widening. I thought about how it applied to the marriage act. The groom penetrates the bride's temple body, and her blood is shed as the hymen is opened. The opening of her temple veil is done precisely where his own covenant blood had earlier been shed. In the process of their being united into one, each meets the covenant requirement of having given blood on behalf of the other: The man gave his blood for her; she gave her blood to him. This parallels Jesus and His bride, the church. Jesus shed His blood for the bride in order to redeem her. (See Colossians 1:20; Hebrews 13:20–21.) His bride, the church, gives her blood back to Him when she shows her love through martyrdom (see Revelation 12:11).

The New Testament makes the covenant meaning of Old Testament circumcision more beautiful than that which Israel understood. The death and resurrection of Jesus transformed circumcision into an experience of the heart. It is no longer limited to the outer body.

> He is not a Jew who is one outwardly, nor is circumcision that which is outward in the flesh; but he is a Jew who is one inwardly; and circumcision is that of the heart, in the Spirit, not in the letter; whose praise is not from men but from God (Rom. 2:28–29).

> For in Christ Jesus neither circumcision nor uncircumcision avails anything, but a new creation (Gal. 6:15).

Being far more than a physical cutting of the outer flesh, it is now man's inner being, his heart, that bears the sign of covenant. No longer an earthly symbol, circumcision is now a heavenly reality, bringing ultimate relationship with the Creator-Father.

On this subject of rings, I wish to comment on the covenant meaning of the golden bells and pomegranates decorating the garment of Israel's high priest. (See

Exodus 28:33–34.) The fruit and bells on the hem of his robe undoubtedly symbolize the fruit and gifts of the Spirit. (See Galatians 5:22; Ephesians 5:9.) As High Priest, Jesus is prophetically portrayed in ancient tabernacle worship and bears both fruit and gifts. (See Hebrews 3:1.) To be like Him, we must bear the same. Christians who reject spiritual gifts are ripping them off the garment of Jesus. Don't do it. When viewed from the bottom, the bell is usually a round ring. In scriptural typology, that golden ring may be as wide as the rainbow or as small as the scar on a man's body. In either case, it speaks of covenant.

Failure Under Apollos; Success Under Paul

Apollos was the pastor of a small, struggling congregation at Ephesus when he left temporarily to visit Corinth. While away, Paul came to Ephesus and found Apollos' church of twelve male disciples with their wives and children. Paul immediately recognized powerlessness in this flock. (See Acts 18:24–19:20.) In spite of Apollos having excellent credentials for ministry, he was not fulfilling the true New Testament example. He was stung with failure while Paul was not. Both men were called of God, both equally loved the Lord, and each possessed vast knowledge of Scripture. Even so, a major discrepancy existed between their ministries. Paul had power; Apollos did not. Carefully observe these seven facts which Scripture records about Apollos:

1. He was a Jew.
2. An eloquent man.
3. Mighty in Scripture.
4. Instructed in the way of the Lord.
5. Fervent in spirit.
6. Taught accurately the things of the Lord.

7. He knew only the water baptism of John—nothing about Jesus' baptism in the Spirit.

When Paul recognized spiritual powerlessness in the Ephesians, he asked the all-revealing question, "Did you receive the Holy Spirit when you believed?" They responded, "We have not so much as heard whether there is a Holy Spirit." This tragic ignorance existed because Apollos knew only the baptism of John. He knew nothing about the baptism in the Holy Spirit and consequently left his congregation in that same theological vacuum. Paul immediately instructed the Ephesians about the Holy Spirit's empowering, and when he "laid hands on them, the Holy Spirit came upon them, and they spoke with tongues and prophesied" (Acts 19:6).

Under Apollos' ministry, the church at Ephesus accomplished absolutely nothing to awaken the city. It demonstrated no kingdom power, remained spiritually paralyzed, and except for the local synagogue, its presence was virtually unknown. In that state, the congregation had no effective witness, made no impact on the people, was no threat to "powers, principalities, rulers of the darkness of this world." Instead, the dark cloud of paganism gripped the land with unchallenged control. The Temple of Diana, or Artemis, already famous as the greatest of all seven wonders of the ancient world, dominated the area. It was in the shadow of this formidable enemy that this minuscule church, virtually powerless and unknown, lay dormant.

That changed when Paul arrived. When he came on the scene, Ephesus experienced a kingdom of God earthquake. Paul was not the power, but he was the instrument for that shaking. He merely provided the window through which the power roared. Apollos and twelve other windows were already present in Ephesus, but *they had never been opened.*

Paul's first mission in the city was not to attack the goddess Diana. Not at all. His *first mission* was to impart to the church the power of the Holy Spirit. In the identical fashion that Ananias earlier laid hands on him in Damascus "that [he might] receive [his] sight and be filled with the Holy Spirit" (Acts 9:17), Paul laid hands on the Ephesian believers with the same hell-shattering results.

After "the Holy Spirit came upon them" (Acts 19:6), the power of the gospel blew the city apart. A riot followed. These twelve disciples and their families became a spiritual Hercules that multiplied into a hundred, then five thousand, then tens of thousands. Thousands more were converted, the church exploded in power, the Temple of Diana was ultimately emptied and destroyed. In time, the city of Ephesus became a Christian citadel known throughout the Roman world. For centuries the fire of the Ephesian revival burned out of control.

What caused such a revolutionary transformation? It was not Paul. It was the power of the Holy Spirit working through Paul. Be aware of this important point of theology: That power did not come to Paul on the Damascus road when he met Jesus. Not at all. It came in the Damascus room. That day, under the hands of Ananias, Paul was filled with the Holy Spirit. (See Acts 9:17.) Identically, the believers in Ephesus were already born again when Paul arrived; they had a Damascus road encounter with Jesus. But not until Paul laid hands on them did they experience their Damascus room baptism in the Holy Spirit. That event anointed them with kingdom power. From that moment on, Ephesian paganism was doomed. One destiny awaited it: It would bow its knees to the Lordship of Jesus Christ.

How appropriate that Paul should write to the Corinthians, "I will come to you shortly... and I will know, not the word of those who are puffed up, but the power." (1 Cor. 4:19). Eloquence, might, fervency, accuracy in the things of God—these things did not impress Paul. He had already witnessed the failure of Christianized wisdom. This fact prompted him to write that God has made us sufficient as "ministers of the new covenant, not of the letter but of the Spirit; for the letter kills, but the Spirit gives life" (2 Cor. 3:6).

It matters not how eloquent one may be, how mighty in the Scripture, how instructed in the ways of the Lord, how accurately he teaches the things of God, how fervent he is in spirit, or how many degrees hang on his office wall, he may still be spinning his theological wheels, accomplishing minimal results, until he has been filled with the Holy Spirit. That is not my word; that is God's Word. If it were true of Apollos and the Ephesians, I can guarantee, it is equally true of us today.

There is not a city on this planet, be it Ephesus, Peking, Mexico City, Washington, Cape Town, New Delhi, Hong Kong or Moscow, that can successfully resist such a dam burst of the power of God. Fifty years ago, that dam burst happened unexpectedly in Argentina under the ministry of Tommy Hicks and has since turned Latin America upside down. Daily, more than twenty thousand new believers are coming to Christ in Latin America. God grant that someone becomes the North American voice who similarly shakes this continent to its core.

For that to happen, the church must jointly pray, "God Almighty! Your kingdom come, Your will be done in earth as it is being done in heaven. Holy Spirit, wake up every powerless Apollos, change each into another Paul, shake us, stir us, challenge us, fill us. More importantly, send us forth in Your power to bring the nations to their knees. Glorify Jesus in every city of our land!"

Chapter Six

History That Encourages: God Used Others Like You

In 1949, Tommy Hicks, an unknown American evangelist, walked up to the palace of Dictator Juan Peron in Buenos Aires, Argentina, and asked to speak to the president. The armed guard at the gate laughed at him. The visitor had no credentials except the claim that God had sent him. The purpose of his visit with Mr. Peron, he explained, was to request use of the fifteen-thousand seat Atlantic Stadium for an evangelistic and healing crusade.

The soldier was not interested in the stadium or the crusade, but he was very interested in healing. At that moment he was in serious pain and interrupted Tommy Hicks to ask, "Can God heal me?" He then explained his need. Without hesitating, Tommy took hold of the young man's hands and prayed. Immediately the power of God went through him. Every evidence of his disease, including pain, disappeared. He was healed. Wide-eyed, the soldier gasped, "Come back tomorrow." He assured Tommy, "You will see the president!" In that strange moment on the steps of the presidential palace, God opened a door for the gospel to invade the whole of South America. That young soldier's healing was only the first in a long line of miraculous works which the Holy Spirit would do.

The background of that wonderful event was that a few *evangelicos* had invited Brother Hicks to conduct a crusade in Argentina. They hoped to draw a crowd of twenty-five hundred but had no aspirations for more than that. When Tommy suggested they acquire use of the Atlantic Stadium, the other pastors laughed. This was Catholic Argentina, not the United States! Less than 2 percent of the population was Protestant. There was a strong military government. Peron was a dictator who jealously monitored every public meeting. His wife, Evita, was suspected of being deeply involved with the occult and was not a friend of the gospel. It was for those reasons that Tommy Hicks was alone when he appeared at the presidential palace. The other pastors were afraid to go with him.

The next afternoon when Tommy returned he was quickly escorted into the spacious presidential office and stood facing Mr. Peron. A large desk was between them. Mr. Peron asked him to be seated, and Tommy immediately explained that God had sent him to Argentina to hold a salvation and healing crusade. They needed a large stadium plus free radio and press coverage. President Peron listened intently. Suddenly, he interrupted the evangelist, rose quickly to his feet, and said, "Can God heal me?" He stared at the young American, asking again, "Can God heal me?" Though the Argentine public did not know it, President Peron suffered from an ugly eczema that was slowly disfiguring his body and causing a serious threat to his life. Doctors had been unable to help. Tommy quickly reached across the desk and said, "Give me your hands." Mr. Peron responded, and as Tommy prayed, the power of the Holy Spirit went through the president's body. With everyone in the room looking on, Juan Peron's skin suddenly became as soft and clear as a baby's. *"¡Dios mio! ¡Estoy sanado!"* Peron exclaimed. *"My God! I am healed!"* And he was.

Tommy Hicks had no difficulty getting the Atlantic Stadium, the free news coverage—or the people. Immediately the Holy Spirit began to move. Enormous crowds packed the stadium until there was no more room. Ushers soon worked twelve-hour shifts; bleachers were filled half-a-day before services began. Parking lots around the stadium were jammed; additional loudspeakers were installed to broadcast sermons to the crowds outside. Peasants walked for miles from the surrounding countryside and camped under trees. Trains and busses were packed. Visitors flew in from other Latin American countries. Though it was winter, every available seat, aisle and ramp was filled. In many cases, people stood for hours. Others slept all night on the metal walkways to be sure of getting a spot.

The Holy Spirit fell in power, and thousands upon thousands were healed. Many thousands more were saved as God began revival in Argentina that has no parallel in modern times. When the crowds outgrew the Atlantic Stadium, they moved to the 180,000-seat Huracan Stadium, the largest in the country, and immediately overflowed it. Until that time, this stadium had never been filled. No sporting event or political rally had ever been able to draw enough people to occupy it. God changed that. He turned Argentina upside down and planted the tree of the gospel deeply in its soil. God's hand was "stretched out over all the nations" (Isa. 14:26); there was no turning it back.

In a short time, every available Bible in Argentina was

sold—fifty-five thousand copies. New ones were ordered from other countries. An English newspaper in Buenos Aires reported that the congregation grew to more than two hundred thousand. The sister of Bolivia's vice president brought her children to be healed. The wife of Argentina's vice president began prayer meetings and Bible studies in her home. Catholic hierarchy went into panic. One of the nation's provincial governors was healed. A nationally known Spanish publisher who had spent his life in a wheelchair leaped from it and ran around before an astonished crowd.

Magazines and newspapers daily printed articles and photographs of invalids and wheelchair patients walking. These were not fakes. Some were people everyone knew. God moved in Argentina in a sovereign display of His power and healing mercy. Children were healed. Old people were healed. The rich, the poor, Indian peasants, and Spanish aristocrats found themselves praying together and weeping for joy. *Jesus was alive. He was real.* Soldiers, policemen, others who came to the meetings only to serve as escorts, reverently dropped to their knees when they saw the power of God sweeping through the people. Jesus was not only alive, but He was in Argentina. *And they knew it.* Today South America is aflame.

Several years ago I preached in Argentina and met people who witnessed that historic outpouring of the Holy Spirit. They assured me *it was real,* and they recounted the entire story as I have told it. In the city of Resistencia, I spoke in one of the congregations of Pastor Omar Cabrerra's three-hundred-thousand-member church. No stadium in Argentina is large enough to accommodate the whole membership. This church, plus numerous others with thirty thousand members or more, are outgrowths of the Tommy Hicks crusade. Fifty years after the Holy Spirit's visitation,

Argentina is still burning with the power of Jesus Christ.

While in Argentina I had lunch at the national capitol building with a born-again believer who is one of many Spirit-filled men and women now holding executive positions in national politics. But that was not as important as my visit to another spot. Before leaving Argentina, I went to the presidential palace, Casa Rosada, across from the capitol in downtown Buenos Aires, and stood on the steps near where Tommy Hicks talked with the guard that momentous day. My heart pounded with gratitude as I thanked the Holy Spirit for slipping the "bracelet of healing" on that young man's body. That was the event that ignited South America; in that moment a massive circumcision uncovered a continent. Standing there, I was overcome with awe for our wonderful God who loves dictators the same as peasants and pours apostolic power into unknown preachers. With tears, I thanked Him for vibrating a nation and sending shock waves across Latin America.

The Holy Spirit's Move Through Chinese Baptists

Very few Southern Baptists in the United States today know of the Holy Spirit's move in their missions in China in the early 1930s. An American missionary working there, Mary K. Crawford of the North China Mission, wrote extensively of her own baptism in the Spirit and the dramatic effects that the experience brought to Chinese Baptists. The amazing revival underway in China today is due in part to His work among Southern Baptists in the 1930s. Miss Crawford wrote:

> I came to China in 1923 and for several years did my best to learn the language and witness the best I could for the Lord. I continually felt that I was powerless, and

the millions of unsaved people all around made me feel helpless. In 1927, while most of the missionaries were refugeeing in Chefoo, I had a conference with a missionary who asked me if I had been "filled with the Holy Spirit." Her question puzzled me, as I had never heard a question like that put so straightforward. But that question set me to thinking, praying and searching the Scriptures... While in prayer alone at Laichow a few weeks later, I asked the Lord to give me the fullness of the Holy Spirit. After two or three hours of prayer and meditation, He gave me *a most blessed experience.*

In 1931, God began to work mightily in Shantung... My whole being seemed to be going through a great change. It seemed like a strong electric current was going through my body... I was absolutely unafraid and conscious that it was God's Holy Spirit's work. He took right hold of me and shook me physically as I would shake a rag, then He opened my mouth so wide that my jaw bones seemed like they would break. The room was filled with wind, and it literally rushed into me until I felt that I would burst. This happened four or five times. Then a great burst of joyous laughter that was different from any laughter that I had ever experienced came right from deep inside me. This happened over and over.

To make a long story short, from September 1931 to June 1932, at least twenty-four missionaries and many Chinese leaders had a definite experience of the baptism in the Holy Spirit and were rejoicing all through the year as they saw new light and life coming into the churches.

In our annual Missionary Conference here these last few days someone exclaimed: "Oh, that our Baptist people at home could hear and see what has come to our ears and eyes these past months!" ...Numbers of Christians and churches are being revived... Sick are being healed, devils cast out, men and women, boys and girls are preaching with a power hitherto not known... Average Christians became dissatisfied, put themselves on the altar anew, were filled with the Spirit... They have a new joy in the Lord and a vigor in their work hitherto not known...

In the revival here in Hwanghsien last spring the North China Baptist Theological Seminary and Bible School came in for a great blessing. Every one of the faculty got a distinct blessing, and nearly everyone of them was filled with the Holy Spirit. It has made a new school... It is a new day for us. Every month or so all the churches and out-stations have had special revivals held by missionaries or special evangelists, and the results have been greater than many previous years put together. One blessed result of the outpouring of the Spirit is that He sends people to ask the Way.

July 15, 1932... There have been between two and three thousand conversions in Pingtu county this year. No less than one thousand have been baptized. At another village God's Spirit seemed to fall upon the people like fire. They fell before Him, asking for forgiveness and salvation. During a meeting the speaker arose from prayer only to see his congregation leaving the house. He found that old Sister Kiao, who had been sick and was carried to the meeting had gotten up, walked out, and was on her way home, a third of a mile away, to tell her family she was healed. The village people marvel, for she had not walked for twenty years and was known to be helpless. She is still walking, and with others, is praising God.

Mrs. Loa had been a paralytic for eighteen years... During the revival at her own church, she was prayed for twice, her faith was strengthened, and she felt better. About a month later she was brought to Pingtu, and on December 10, 1931, was prayed for according to James 5. She arose immediately and walked from the missionary's home where the prayer took place over to the church, and has been walking ever since. A telegram was sent to her husband in Chefoo, but he could not believe the good news and thought it must be mesmerism. He had spent much money on a cure for his wife and had been told by one foreign doctor and two Chinese doctors, both graduates of foreign mission hospitals of repute, that there was no cure for his wife. He knew that his wife's lower limbs were drawn up, large at the joints, but small as little sticks with no muscles at all. Nevertheless, the husband put aside his work and came home doubting, but his joy was to be met at the gate by his wife who had walked out to meet him.

—MARY K. CRAWFORD
"THE SHANTAUG REVIVAL"

Revival Falls on a Lonely Scottish Island

One of the great visitations of the Holy Spirit in this century occurred in the 1950s on the extreme northern coast of Scotland under the preaching of Duncan Campbell. Though its effect was confined to a small area in the Hebrides Islands, the power that exploded upon the island of Berneray was identical to that of the Book of Acts. That move of God began in a barn with a man named Hector McKennon sprawled out in the straw, praying.

There were only two churches on the island of Berneray, and both had been closed for years. The last pastor died. Others quit coming. Hector was the only remaining elder. The church deaths came about because passion for Jesus had been replaced with doctrines about Jesus. Finally, people lost interest in doctrine. Seemingly, Hector was the only one determined to bring spiritual life back to the island's desolation. His wife told of the memorable day he locked himself in the barn, refusing to come out until heaven answered. Several times she walked to the door, heard her husband thrashing about, groaning before the Lord, "I don't know where he is, Lord, but You do!" She heard him plead, "Send Duncan Campbell to Berneray! Send Duncan Campbell to Berneray!"

Duncan was one of the great spiritual forces in the British Isles. He too was a Gaelic-speaking Highlander who came to the Lord in a phenomenal conversion before the first World War. That conversion had been accompanied by a powerful anointing of the Holy Spirit. Later, on a French battlefield of the war, Duncan lay severely wounded in the path of a cavalry charge, and he was trampled by the horses. Finally rescued, he was taken to a field hospital for surgery. The pain was incredible. On the operating table, the prayer he shouted in Gaelic was not for healing but for holiness: "Lord, make me as holy as a saved sinner can be! Make me as holy as a saved sinner can be!" Though his Scottish tongue was not understood by a single person in the tent, the cry brought such power of God upon him that seven men were saved.

Through the years, the anointing intensified as God "confirmed His word with signs following." Duncan hungered for heaven and once during crisis sought a greater empowering of the Holy Spirit. Of the event, he said, "As I lay there, God, the Holy Ghost, came upon me. Wave after wave came rolling over me until the love of God swept through me like a mighty river!... I was so wrought upon by the Holy Ghost that I cried—and I laughed—and I prayed."

Hector McKennon's heart grieved for Berneray to experience the ministry of Duncan Campbell. As the day passed, Hector continued praying. Three times his wife went to the door listening.

At ten o'clock that night, hundreds of miles away, Duncan Campbell sat on the platform of England's largest Christian gathering, the Bangor Convention. He was to be the final speaker. At precisely ten o'clock two amazing things happened: Duncan heard the voice of his Friend, the Holy Spirit, tell him to leave the convention. "Leave now." The message was surprising; in a sense, troubling. He thought the Holy Spirit had wanted him at the convention. At the same moment Hector came running out of the barn yelling, "He's coming! He's coming! God said he's coming. He'll be here tomorrow night!"

Duncan learned early in his Christian walk not to strive with the Holy Spirit—but he needed to be certain. Without others knowing what was happening, he prayed for confirmation. When the answer came, he turned abruptly to the convention's chairman, "I have to leave," he explained. "God is sending me to the Island of Berneray."

Over protest, Duncan flew to Glasgow, took the train to Stornoway, and finally traveled by car to the ferry. Arriving at Berneray the next day, uninvited and unannounced, he stopped a boy, asked about the churches, learned the name of the island's only elder, and said, "Go tell Hector McKennon that Duncan Campbell has arrived." A short time later the boy hurried back saying, "Elder McKennon was expecting you today and has arranged for you to stay with his brother. He has called a meeting at the church at nine o'clock tonight, and you are to address it."

Duncan knew he had correctly heard his heavenly Friend, even though nothing significant happened in the evening service. At 11:00 that night, the congregation spilled out of the church and starting walked downhill in the moonlight to their homes. Suddenly, Hector jerked Duncan's arm, snatched off his hat, and said, "Stand, Mr. Campbell. God has come! God has come! See what is happening!" Duncan looked at the scene on the hill below them. The wind of God was blowing upon the people, scattering them like leaves among the heather. They were falling under the power of the Holy Spirit, wailing, crying to God. The old, the young, men and women, dropped on that bleak hillside and remained there until four o'clock in the morning. Their repentance and grief over sin groaned out of them into the cold North Sea air. Other islanders who had not attended the service came looking for loved ones, found them weeping in the heather, were overcome by the Spirit's presence, and joined them among the rocks. God had come to the Hebrides. That was the beginning.

A few nights later, a group met to pray in an old house in another village where the people were still unrepentant. God's power had not fallen on them. It was after midnight when a man suddenly sprang to the center of the room, raised his hand and called loudly to God, "You promised to pour Your Spirit on a dry and thirsty land, and You're not doing it!" (see Isaiah 44:3). Waving his hand toward the ceiling, he shouted boldly, "I challenge You! Do it!"

Instantly, according to Duncan, "The stone farm house *shook like a leaf*" as the power of God slammed upon the village. Everyone at the prayer meeting ran out into the night, looking around; all the houses within sight had lights coming on; the entire village had been suddenly awakened. Duncan hurried to the nearest dwelling, went in the back door and found husband and wife face-down on the kitchen floor, seeking the Lord. At the next house, he saw the same. And again, at the next. Revival had fallen upon the town.

The power of God quickly fell upon other villages until the area was ablaze with holy fire. This was true New Testament revival. Even the shaking of the building paralleled two events in the Book of Acts, Acts 4:31 and 16:26. More importantly, the people were changed. (See Acts 2:37.) Why had it happened? Hector McKennon was a man of unrelenting prayer; Duncan Campbell was a man of unrelenting obedience. Hector pulled the power out of heaven and down upon his island. Duncan was the window through which the power roared. Their combination was unstoppable. Both stood, feet on earth, faces in heaven.[1]

What happened in the Hebrides is the kind of revival for which the church in our day must pray! Anything less is insufficient. Good as our "church meetings" are, most are only feathers thrown into the wind. We need New-Testament, Book-of-Acts outpourings of the Holy Spirit. Our church pews would not be vacant, altar calls would not be empty if we dared pray with the authority of this Scottish man who seized heaven and shook hell. We need sovereign, sinner-quaking, city-shaking revival! You can become that Hector or Duncan for your church and town. All God seeks is a willing heart. He does not want your ability; He wants only your availability.

Pilgrims and Puritans Experience the Power

When the Pilgrims fled England for America, they left behind one of the bright stars of the Puritan movement. That was Pastor John Robinson, who helped guide Puritans through years of political and religious turmoil. He planned to join his flock in the New World. That never happened. Six years after their arrival in North America, John Robinson died, still in England. His death was a grievous blow. John was in his forties, and the cause of truth desperately needed him.

In reality, the Pilgrims were never without his guidance. Not only did they have his written sermons and numerous letters, but one special message would always be engraved upon their hearts. It was the farewell address that he delivered at the time of their sailing. In that message, the Holy Spirit gave him a prophetic word that still challenges the church four centuries later. Examine it carefully:

> I charge you before God and before His blessed angels, that you follow me no further than you have seen me follow the Lord Jesus Christ. If God reveal anything to you by any other instrument of His (another minister), be as ready to receive it as ever you were to receive any truth by my ministry: for I am verily persuaded, I am very confident, the Lord hath more truth yet to break forth out of His holy Word.
>
> For my part, I cannot sufficiently bewail the condition of the reformed churches, who are come to a full stop in religion and will go at present no further than the instruments of their first reformation. The Lutherans cannot be drawn to go beyond what Luther saw: whatever part of his will our good God has imparted and revealed unto Calvin, they will rather die than embrace it. And the Calvinists, you see, stick fast where they were left by that great man of God; who yet saw not all things. This is a misery much to be lamented; for though they were burning and shining lights in their times, yet they penetrated not into the whole counsel of God: but were they now living, they would be as willing to embrace further light, as that which they first received.”[2]

The separate messages in this quote are astounding. Some of the radical concepts of truth and liberty that were birthed in Colonial America came from the influence of this man. For example:

1. "The Lord hath more truth yet to break forth out of His holy Word."

John Robinson did not believe that theologians of his day had exhausted the mine of God's written truth. Rather, he was convinced they had only broken through the topsoil of an inexhaustible quarry of divine gold.

2. "The reformed churches... are come to a full stop in religion and will go at present, no further than the instruments of their first reformation." They "stick fast where they were left by that great man of God."

Though Robinson did not regard himself as either Lutheran or Calvinist, he grieved that they had become "closed-door" denominations. This attitude was in direct opposition to their founders. Martin Luther and John Calvin had been willing to accept the reality of "more truth" breaking out of God's Word. That had been the very enticement that forced their pressing deeper into the truth of Scripture. In both cases, their efforts had been rewarded by the sudden burst of new revelation. Their followers, by contrast, stuck "fast where they were left by those great men of God." Observe that Robinson used the expression "first reformation." By that, he expected God would lead them into a progressive, ongoing revelation with a second, and perhaps a third, stage of development.

3. "Whatever part of His will our good God has imparted and revealed unto Calvin, the Lutherans will rather die than embrace it."

The religious trap which Luther and Calvin zealously fought to escape, that is, the "polarization, isolation and stagnation" of traditionalism, was being frantically defended by their own disciples. Robinson saw the church's return to the bondage of new-style Protestant tradition as a "misery much to be lamented."

4. Though Luther and Calvin "were burning and shining

lights in their times, yet they penetrated not into the whole counsel of God."

Luther knew he had not explored the "heights and depths" of God; Calvin also knew it. The ultimates of revelation still shone beyond these men. And sadly, denominational Christianity, for the most part, is still polarized around itself, isolated from revelation God has imparted to its neighbors. Religious inbreeding is always the slow death of Christian groups which reject "more truth" from God.

5. Were Luther and Calvin "now living, they would be as willing to embrace further light, as that which they first received."

This is not an unfounded statement to make of these men. They *were* willing to embrace further light when the opportunity came. And if they had done it the first time, they would do it again. That simple fact of their willingness engraved their names in history. Until recently, the mindset of most denominationalism has been, "We can only believe and do what our ancestors believed and did." That is the very attitude which the Reformers sought to escape, not to preserve. Had that narrow principle been their guide there would have been no Reformation and the Bible would still be a closed, unknown book.

This "misery much to be lamented," that is, the refusal of Christians to accept what God has revealed to other believers, is now changing. Baptists and Brethren are receiving "more truth" about the baptism and gifts of the Holy Spirit. So are Methodists and Mennonites. Presbyterians and Pentecostals are learning from each other. John Robinson would be pleased. God has "more truth" breaking forth out of His holy Word. The current emphasis on the work of the Holy Spirit is part of it. To all who choose truth over tradition, the world says, thank you!

God's Move in Moravia

In 1987, on the 250th anniversary of its founding, I visited New Herrnhut Moravian Church on the island of St. Thomas in the Virgin Islands. Visiting this mountain-side shrine and the jungle overhanging its cemetery impacted my life in a way I will carry to my grave. There are churches in the western hemisphere much older than Herrnhut, but none can compare with its special history. In 1737, the first missionaries of the modern era came to this jungle island to bring the gospel to African slaves. When Leonard Dober and David Nitschmann stepped ashore on St. Thomas, Bibles in hand, they struck the symbolic gong that awoke a slumbering evangelical church and sent the mission movement around the world. From the vibrations of that gong, in our century alone, more than one hundred million new believers in Latin America and the Caribbean have come to Christ. The story behind these young men and women is the crown jewel in the modern mission movement.

In the early 1700s, a congregation of some three hundred Hussites, Anabaptists, Calvinists, disciples of Swingle, Schwenkfold, and other nonconformists, sought refuge on the estate of Count Zinzendorf in Saxony, East Germany. Like the count, who was only twenty-seven years old, most members of the community were young; all had fled persecution in other parts of Europe. In the beginning, they quarreled over doctrines of baptism, predestination, holiness, etc., until the count encouraged them to concentrate on their love for Jesus. It was the cross, not doctrines about the cross, he reminded them, that brought their redemption. In that understanding, they united in covenant agreement and began seeking the Lord in travailing prayer. This is what happened:

1. Tuesday, August 5, 1727. Count Zinzendorf spent the

entire night in watching and prayer. Herrnhut means "the Lord's watch."

2. Sunday, August 10, 1727, at noon. When Pastor Rothe preached, the congregation fell under the power of the Holy Spirit.

3. Wednesday, August 13, 1727, at morning communion. The power of God came upon the community in such shattering force that men working in the fields ten miles away were stricken under the shock of it. Even today, its impact is without parallel in modern Christian history.

4. Tuesday, August 26, 1727. The children were anointed with three hours of anguished intercession.

5. Wednesday, August 27, 1727. At the initiation of the children, Herrnhut began a prayer meeting that lasted night and day, without stopping, for an amazing one hundred years.

That century-long prayer meeting of laboring, travailing, intercession, from 1727 to 1827, birthed the modern mission movement. One hundred years after it closed, and long after the original members of Herrnhut were dead, every Protestant denomination engaged in carrying the gospel to the heathen did so because of that century of Moravian praying.

In 1737, ten years after the Holy Spirit's fall, the first Moravians left for the island of St. Thomas. During that decade of self-crucifying preparation, ripening of grace, they sought the Spirit's endowing for the work. They well knew that once in the Virgin Islands they too might become slaves. Still they determined to go. When the day came to make the choice as to who would be the first to leave, Scripture quotations were written on slips of paper and placed in a box. After agonizing prayer, each person drew out one of the notes. Whether one stayed in Moravia or went to the mission field was determined by the instruction he withdrew (Acts 1:26). With heart racing, one of the young men opened his paper and read the words,

Send the lad with me, and we will arise and go (Gen. 43:8).

With that message in hand, Leonard Dober and David Nitschmann left home, walking more than one hundred miles to Copenhagen, Denmark. At the port, they found passage to the islands by working as deckhands on a ship. Arriving on St. Thomas, the conditions in which they found the slaves drove them to their knees. The Lutheran church was the state religion on the islands, but blacks were not allowed to go near the buildings. One slave who tried to hear the message of Jesus through the church window was punished by having his ear cut off.

Frederich Martin soon joined Leonard and David in St. Thomas but was imprisoned in the fortress dungeon at Charlotte Amalie. Through a tiny, barred window of this 1671-built fort, he continued preaching to listeners outside. These men were soon followed by Tobias Leopold, who went to the island of St. Croix. Slave churches established by these missionaries still survive on St. Thomas, St. John, St. Croix and surrounding islands.

Moravian missionaries quickly flooded out of Germany like water rushing over a spillway. Within twenty-five years, more than two hundred preachers went to every continent on earth, including Greenland. With the zeal of first-century believers, these Spirit-baptized youths took the flame of the Holy Spirit to every country in North and South America, much of Asia and Africa. Only a few came to the United States; most preferring un-evangelized areas. Of the eighteen missionaries who went to the Virgin Islands, half perished of tropical disease the first year. Tobias Leopold died on St. Croix, shouting the message of the gospel.[3]

On that first trip to St. Thomas, I wanted to touch every part of the island those men had known. To do that, I explored every dungeon in the old fort, feeling its stone walls, praying about Frederich Martin, the prisoner who shouted the gospel from behind these walls. The big impact came later, walking between tombstones in the jungle below Herrnhut church. In my heart, I heard voices of young men and women from 250 years in the past. I felt unworthy to touch their burial ground, and I wept aloud, yelling my thanks for what they did. It didn't matter who heard me. I *wanted* hell to hear me. I *wanted* my own heart to hear me. Most important of all, I *wanted* God to hear me say I would die unfulfilled unless I experienced the same power of the Holy Spirit that those young Moravians knew. Suddenly, I had Jesus' reply: "How much more will your heavenly Father give the Holy Spirit to those who ask Him!" (Luke 11:13).

Standing there alone in that jungle graveyard, I was overwhelmed by an amazing presence of the Holy Spirit. He was all around me. It was the same wonderful Friend who had come upon Tobias, Frederich, Leonard, David and others that blessed August day in Moravia. In that moment, the dirt on my feet seemed too holy to wipe off. But it wasn't dirt I carried out of the cemetery. I took with me the knowledge that the same Holy Spirit who empowered the Moravians was willing to empower men like me. And I saw Him begin that work in astonishing ways.

Moravia's Effect on Baptists and Methodists

Soon after the Holy Spirit's move in Moravia, He began a new work in the British Isles. The early part of the 1700s witnessed the rise of John and Charles Wesley, and the

101

Methodist movement was born. The brothers were deeply affected by the ministry of the Moravian pastor, Peter Bohler, in London. During one of Bohler's sermons, John experienced "justifying faith" and stepped into an empowered relationship with Jesus Christ.

Few other eras in world history have impacted mankind evangelically as did that blazing period. As a result, millions of believers were won to Christ. It not only woke up a slumbering, tradition-choked church but sent a shock wave around the world. Christians were revived, and the course of nations changed. Many of our greatest Christian hymns were birthed during those wonderful years.

Later in the century, the Baptists were shaken by the voices of William Carey, John Ryland and others who had come under the power of Moravian preaching. These daring young men initiated the first Baptist mission work to the heathen. In one of their meetings, when senior ministers loudly opposed them, they dropped a Moravian magazine on the table and pleaded for support. In both cases—the Wesleys and Carey—fierce opposition rose against them because the work was new. Even so, Carey finally sailed for India, enduring years of horrendous trials, until he had successfully planted the tree of the gospel in Hindu soil. Today there are an estimated twenty-five million Christians in India.[4]

For nearly two centuries, England blossomed under this fresh outpouring of the Holy Spirit. Genuine, New Testament evangelism touched and changed millions of lives. Later, however, things changed. Fervor in the churches cooled, hardening again, and congregations became much like they had been before. Christians fell back into religion as a replacement for spirituality. Historically, the Holy Spirit's move in the church has been characterized by the following progression:

1. Inspiration
2. Evangelization
3. Organization
4. Stagnation

At the point of stagnation, there has usually been an outcry for inspiration. Re-birthing consequently follows, and the cycle repeats itself. Historically, and without exception, those Christian bodies who rejected God's call to evangelize the heathen died in their own stagnation. Though once powerful and strong, they have vanished from the scene of spiritual influence. God will not tolerate self-centeredness and religious greed. Groups who exist for themselves quickly die by themselves. There is no exemption from this rule.

Today, Wesley would be horrified at the unbelief permitted in parts of his own Methodist church. Thankfully, the charismatic renewal is changing that. William Carey would have special reason to grieve:

In England, Carey's old stone church building was bulldozed, and a Hindu Temple built in its place.

The historic building in which William Carey preached, prayed and wept for God to send him to India, came under the wrecking ball. India had come to England. Why did it happen? How could the virtual shrine of the Baptist Foreign Mission Movement come under the ax? The answer is simple: The Baptists were gone. Like hundreds of other church buildings in England and on the Continent, no one attended the services. More alarming than that, however, is the reality that there are more Muslims in England today than there are Methodists and Baptists combined.

And that has happened in a historic *Christian* nation.

In 1699, the Islamic invasion of Europe was stopped outside the gates of Vienna after 2½ *centuries* of bloody fighting.

The victory that saved Europe from death by Muslim swords came only at the cost of thousands of lives and the urgent wailing of Christian prayers. Every congregation in Europe was on its face in frantic prayer for deliverance. Today the invasion has taken on a different tactic—and without an outcry. Mosques and Hindu temples are sprouting up as far north as the tip of Scotland. More frightening, the conversion rate of new believers in English churches is less than 2 percent while the Muslim rate of conversion is 15 percent. In 1699, every church in Europe was praying. Today, with the new invasion, that is not happening. For the most part, churches are strangely silent. Concern, however, is not about Hindus or Muslims in England or America; concern is about the church on both sides of the Atlantic. Radical change and renewal *are* needed.

Here is the good news for Britain: More than one hundred thousand charismatic home groups in England are currently teaching, witnessing and praying for revival to sweep the British Isles. Old doors are opening to a new message. As a result, many Anglican churches are experiencing renewal. When I preached at London's world-famous Westminster Chapel, the Holy Spirit moved in an awesome, sovereign demonstration of His presence. Every aisle and floor space was covered with people felled by the Spirit. Some were overcome with riotous laughter; many lay quietly in the "embrace of their loving Father;" while others experienced deliverance from demons. When Cambridge scholar Derek Prince preached in Europe's cathedrals, the same manifestations took place.

Carey's church *building* may be gone, bulldozed, but the Holy Spirit who inspired Carey is *still* here. God has more Wesleys and Careys waiting in the wings. Such men can again wake up the church.

The Fire of American Revival

In the early 1800s, the Holy Spirit fell on a pioneer Presbyterian communion service at Cane Ridge, Kentucky, and sovereignly initiated a fire that changed the entire face of American Christianity. What happened in that outpouring was definitely not usual Presbyterian practice. During the preaching that day, numerous people suddenly began falling to the ground. Some experienced electric-like vibrations; others were jerking. In a short time, noisy repentance, weeping and howling echoed around the meeting house and grounds. No one present had witnessed anything like it before. One spectator described the scene: "At one time I saw at least five hundred swept down in a moment, as if a battery of a thousand guns had been opened upon them..." Pastor Barton W. Stone wrote, "Many, very many, fell down as men slain in battle." Even those who opposed the revival were caught in its power. Some sought to escape but were "struck down as they fled." It affected those "from eight years and upwards, male and female, rich and poor, Whites, Blacks, of every denomination."[5]

George A. Baxter, president of Washington College in Virginia, visited Kentucky at the height of the revival and wrote: "I found Kentucky the most moral place I had ever been in... Upon the whole, I think the revival in Kentucky among the most extraordinary that have ever visited the Church of Christ..."[6]

David Rice, the first Presbyterian minister to settle in Kentucky, told the Kentucky synod in 1803: "A considerable number of persons appears to me to be greatly reformed in their morals. This is undoubtedly the case within the sphere of my particular acquaintance. Yea, some neighborhoods, noted for their vicious and profligate manners, are now as much noted for their piety and good order. Drunkards, profane swearers, liars, quarrelsome persons, etc, are remarkably reformed."[7]

As a result of the Spirit's outpouring, communities were changed from wild, fighting outposts into havens of pious, godly men and women. The Presbyterian synod evaluated the startling nature of the revival and placed its sanction on the event. It recorded, "On the borders of Kentucky and Tennessee, the influence of the Spirit of God seems to have manifested in a very extraordinary manner... Doubtful as the nature of the revival there first appeared... the Assembly do exceedingly rejoice... that its author is God and its effects highly desirable."[8]

What the Presbyterian Assembly had difficulty accepting in the beginning was the unusual physical symptom of the "falling exercise" or what they soon termed being "slain in the Spirit." Others shouted, shook or staggered in a drunken fashion. The unusual physical symptoms were no detraction from the fact that great moral change took place in the people.

The falling experience was first reported in the Gasper River meeting in 1800, but the number "struck down" reached its height at Cane Ridge. One reporter explained: "Some feel the approaching symptoms by being under deep convictions... It comes upon others like an electric shock... They will continue in that state from one hour to twenty-four... often continuing in that state many days." The sight of hundreds of people felled by the power of the Spirit became so common that even the staid Presbyterians were no longer disturbed. One of their documentaries detailed how the fallen were "collected together and laid out in order... which like so many dead corpses, covered a considerable part of the floor. At Mr. Alexander Camble's meeting house a number became affected... On Cabin creek... about sixty persons were struck down... Next Sabbath, on Flemming creek... about one hundred persons were struck down... At Concord... a number were struck down... about one hundred fifty... At Point Pleasant... two hundred fifty were struck down... At Indian Creek... eight hundred struck... at Cane Ridge... three hundred were struck."[9]

The expression, "slain in the spirit," which originated at Cane Ridge, admittedly is an inadequate attempt to identify the experience. No Bible designation was given when Ezekiel, King Saul, Roman soldiers or others "fell" in the Lord's presence. At Pentecost, as well as periods since, the presence of the Spirit definitely caused a "great visible commotion." (See Acts 2:12−14.) As to its purpose, John Wesley said of a notorious sinner who had been suddenly slammed to the earth in one of his meetings, "He came up sobbing and saved." One of the blessings that came from the Holy Spirit's explosion at Cane Ridge was the immediate demand for more pastors. In a 2½-year period, in sparsely settled Kentucky, the Baptists increased by ten thousand new members. In a two-year period, the Methodists added over six thousand. While Presbyterian records are not available, the synod reported "thousands."

The Methodists and Baptists had no difficulty using newly converted circuit riders and farmer preachers; Presbyterians, with their unyielding demand for classical education, were unable to meet the challenge. By the time new pastors returned from seminary, the revival was over. In an attempt to correct that problem, the Cumberland Presbyterian movement was born.

John Wesley said, "When the Church gets on fire, people will come for miles to watch it burn." That happened in Kentucky. People came by the thousands. The church was on fire. In spite of the glory that fell on Kentucky, a dark cloud soon spread across the land. Pastors disagreed over theology. Churches divided. New denominations formed out of the wreckage. Strangely, some became extreme isolationists. Ezra G. Gillett, historian, and David Rice, Presbyterian pastor, were eyewitnesses of good and bad events at Cane Ridge. They wrote:

> Infidelity was laid prostrate but Churches were rent in sunder. The deadness and the lethargy of religion were broken up...[10]
>
> —GILLETT

> [Of that] revival of the spirit and power of Christianity... we have sadly mismanaged it; we have dashed it down and broken it to pieces.[11]
>
> —RICE

While sin was given a deadly blow, lives changed, morality restored, and homes rescued, congregations were also dismantled. Friends became separated. Theological battles arose. New denominations formed from the wreckage. Our question is, "Why would a genuine work of God devastate churches?" Hear me carefully: It was not God's work that destroyed churches. It was the people's stubborn resistance to the Holy Spirit. Religious tradition always resists change. Once tradition is established, it usurps total, absolute, authority over Scripture. Historically, this has been true; altering denominational patterns becomes a heaven-hell struggle. And at Cane Ridge, the Holy Spirit altered everything. He not only demanded change, He demanded *radical* change. Traditional views were overturned. With no forewarning, the frontier church found itself in a tug-of-war between its stable past and a very uncertain future. In the struggle, many forgot that Pentecost had been so radical that the disciples were accused of being drunk. In both places—Jerusalem and Kentucky—skeptics said, "They are full of new wine" (Acts 2:13).

The fact that not everyone who came to Cane Ridge got saved added to the chaos. Drunken brawls, gambling and fights all occurred within earshot of the preaching. Many had no interest in the Lord and were attracted only because of the excitement of the crowd. Fornication, blasphemy, heretical mockery of the preaching went on within the camp. Some worshipers were unable to cope with the non-religious atmosphere that forced its presence onto the revival. In his desperate attempt to stop the hand of God, the devil found a measure of success.

In time, Cane Ridge became history. But it left a permanent mark upon the American church. Without Cane Ridge, the evangelical fire would never have swept North America; the revival permanently changed the face of Protestantism in the United States. Tragically, it left succeeding generations with a vital question to answer: Why have great moves of God been torn apart by the same hands whom they blessed? Hear Jesus' answer: "You reject the commandment of God, that you may keep your tradition" (Mark 7:9).

In 1827, during the outdoor preaching of Adel Sherwood, the Towaliga Baptist Association at Eatonton, Georgia, experienced such an explosion of the Holy Spirit that it left the forest looking like the aftermath of a battle. Ten years later, Baptist churches in that part of the South were still in sweeping revival. The same falling experience happened in the old Kehukee Baptist Association in early America.[12]

Methodists, Presbyterians, Baptists and other evangelicals today who repudiate the unusual works of the Spirit are rejecting their own fathers in the faith. In spite of endless opposition against the Spirit's work, His identical manifestations occurred in the ministries of George

Whitefield, John Wesley, George Fox, the Puritans, the French Huguenots, the Anabaptists, the Waldenses, St. Augustine and others.

All of God's moves have been revolutionary: dividing the Red Sea, bathing Mount Sinai in fire and thunder, opening the earth to swallow the families of Korah, piling up the waters of the Jordan, crashing the walls of Jericho, raising the dead, opening the eyes of the blind with spit and dirt, taking sight from Saul of Tarsus, paralyzing the mouth of Zacharias, killing King Herod, causing disciples at Pentecost to resemble drunks, dropping Ananias and Sapphira dead before the church, wrapping Elymas in darkness. Even with the powerful testimony of Scripture before them, some at Cane Ridge declared the Spirit's work to be mere human emotion. It was this self-inflicted discord that caused David Rice to confess of the revival, "We have sadly mismanaged it; we have dashed it down and broken it to pieces."

American Encounters With the Holy Spirit

A century ago the ministry of Dwight L. Moody shook the nation in a way that continues to vibrate mankind to this day. God changed an ordinary man into one of the great voices in Christian history. Moody himself gives the explanation:

> I began to cry as never before for a greater blessing from God. The hunger increased; I really felt that I did not want to live any longer. I kept on crying all the time that God would fill me with His Spirit. Well, one day in the city of New York—Oh!, what a day, I cannot describe it, I seldom refer to it. It is almost too sacred an experience to name. Paul had an experience of which he never spoke for fourteen years. I can only say, God revealed

Himself to me, and I had such an experience of His love that I had to ask Him *to stay His hand.*[13]

Moody's baptism with the Spirit was so overwhelming, so filling with the glory of heaven, that he felt he would be physically crushed there on the streets of New York. Moody's cry, "God, stay Your hand!" is not unusual for those upon whom the power of the Spirit has fallen. On that historic day, Dwight L. Moody left the spot as a new man and a true New Testament evangelist. What God did for him, He will do for us also who "cry as never before... hunger... do not want to live" unless "filled with the Spirit." Jesus said, "Ask and *you* shall receive."

Following the Book of Acts Example

Authentic moves of the Holy Spirit, whether in individuals such as Moody or communities as Cane Ridge, force this realization upon us: Wonderful as was the sixteenth-century Reformation, *it absolutely is not the model for the twentieth-century church.* Our pattern is the church in the Book of Acts—not medieval Europe. The Reformed churches and leaders were not the originators of Christianity and can *never* become our pattern. Where they differ from the plain, straightforward message of Scripture either in teaching or practice, we must reach beyond them and return to the apostolic example.

The Reformation restored the Word to the church. The current charismatic renewal is restoring the works. Weekly, the renewal movement is establishing fifteen thousand new churches worldwide, as well as bringing new life to old churches. In both camps, Reformed and renewal, approximately eighty thousand conversions take place daily around the world.[14] Both groups have good points and bad, failures and successes. Both are mightily used by God. The role model which the Scripture provided for each is the same: *the first-century church in the Book of Acts.*

In 1991, I was present at the International Charismatic Consultation of World Evangelization at Brighton, England. I witnessed the moment when Archbishop George Carey, who oversees some seventy million Anglican and Episcopalian believers worldwide, gave his endorsement to the charismatic renewal. Sitting there, I was overwhelmed, realizing that in less than thirty years the impact that began in 1964 with Dennis Bennett, an unassuming Episcopal priest at St. Mark's Church in Van Nuys, California, had reached the highest authority of the Church of England. When Bennett received the baptism in the Holy Spirit, he became God's instrument to open the floodgate for charismatic renewal to enter mainline churches. Only God could move that quickly.

Looking around that huge congregation, numbering thousands, I saw Spirit-baptized Christians from more than one hundred nations. Pakistanis, Indonesians, Europeans, Egyptians, Chinese, Americans, Latins, Sri Lankans, Africans, Iraqis and a host of others represented every tradition of Christianity. People who could not speak the others' languages and who were dressed in radically different styles hugged, kissed, rejoiced, like finding long-lost family members. The pastor from a church in Baghdad told that he began with only three people in his congregation; today that number has grown to more than eight hundred. One morning at breakfast, I took a paper napkin and wrote a statement which the press committee released to the English media. It expressed the heart of the congress:

> We are not Christians who have come together and

said, "Let's forget our differences." Rather, we are a group whom the Holy Spirit has called together and said, *"Forgive your differences and correct them."*

As a result of that attitude, modern Christians are on the verge of a new invasion of the Holy Spirit and will see thousands of American churches ablaze with New Testament power. God is returning to His church. A pastor in Pensacola, Florida who warned his congregation against signs and wonders taking place in a neighboring church was suddenly slammed to the floor under the power of the Spirit. God made him experience before his congregation what he had just denied.

Brownsville Assembly of God in Pensacola, Florida, is ablaze with that power. The Toronto Airport Christian Fellowship in Toronto, Canada, exploded in Cane Ridge signs and wonders several years before Pensacola. In London, I visited Holy Trinity, Brompton, an Anglican church that has a world-impacting ministry resulting from its contact with the Toronto Airport Christian Fellowship.

The anointing is contagious. Churches around the world are discovering that fact. Several years before the Brownsville meeting began, the Holy Spirit showed Dr. David Yonggi Cho of Seoul, Korea, the city of Pensacola on a map. "This," He said, "is where the American revival will begin." Prior to that, Dr. Cho was unaware of such a city. Specifically, he was told that after the revival began, it would spread across the nation. Our response to that should be, "Even so, come quickly, Lord Jesus... What we have heard of you in Cane Ridge, do here in this our city" (see Luke 4:23).

Wherever such moves of the Spirit take place, unclean spirits will also manifest. God's power forces them into the open. Such demonstrations disturb churches today just as the demonized man disturbed the Synagogue in Jesus' day.

(See Mark 1:23–27.) Even so, let it happen! If truth disturbs the church, the church needs to be disturbed! Wonderfully, the Toronto and Pensacola meetings are doing that. But someday it is God's will for churches all across America to be described just as David Rice and George Baxter described the Cane Ridge revival: "...Drunkards, profane swearers, quarrelsome persons, are remarkably reformed." "I think the revival... among the most extraordinary that have ever visited the Church of Christ."

Having been to Pensacola, Toronto, Latin America, Africa, and other parts of the world where the Holy Spirit is working, and seeing His presence in my own meetings, it is easy to understand why skeptics use the "new wine/drunken" accusation. People filled with the Holy Spirit sometimes become radically joyous, uninhibited or zealous. Other "drunken" symptoms may occur. Several Church of Christ pastors whose denomination avidly rejects the miraculous moves of the Spirit came to my meetings. Like many others, these men found themselves prostrate on the floor, under the power of God. One lay face down nearly two hours, laughing as if drunk. Today these men are in full gospel ministries, excitedly witnessing the power of God. Medical doctors, college professors, attorneys, other professionals, have identically been felled under the command of God.

At the same time, I have cautioned thousands, "We are seeking the *empowering* of the Holy Spirit. Outward signs happen, but they are not what we are trying to achieve." It is interesting to note that the empowering of the Holy Spirit in the Great Awakening, Cane Ridge, Toronto, and Pensacola revivals, though spread out over nearly three centuries, was accompanied by identical manifestations of the Holy Spirit.

Chapter Seven

Beware the Demon of Unbelief!

Modern Christians love the story of Paul being knocked to the ground on the Damascus Road, blinded, "trembling and astonished, [and saying], 'Lord, what do You want me to do?'" (Acts 9:6). They rejoice when they read about Jesus delivering the maniac of Gadara and the townspeople being "seized with great fear" (Luke 8:37). When the proconsul saw the "dark mist" fall upon Elymas the sorcerer and himself "being astonished at the teaching of the Lord" (Acts 13:12), Bible lovers share in all its excitement.

Christians genuinely believe the New Testament accounts when "fear came upon every soul" (Acts 2:43), or when "great fear came upon all" who heard of the deaths of Ananias and Sapphira. They are grateful when they read how "great fear came upon all the church" (Acts 5:11) or "fear fell on them all" who heard of false exorcists being defeated (Acts 19:16–17). Herod being stricken dead, Zacharias mute, the fortune-telling girl set free from demons—all these are causes to celebrate.

Christians appreciate the fact that the word *astonished* appears nineteen times in the New Testament; *amazed*, sixteen times; *fear*, seventy-four times; and other words of wonderment being equally frequent. Believers today know that the people in the New Testament were in a constant state of awe at the power of God. Unfortunately, that is as far as most Christians today are willing to go. While they are thankful miraculous works accompanied the early church, most want no part of a Book-of-Acts encounter with the Holy Spirit. In spite of that negative attitude, every evangelical congregation still claims Jesus' Great Commission as its doctrinal heart cry:

> Go therefore and make disciples of all the nations, bap-
> tizing them in the name of the Father and of the Son and
> of the Holy Spirit, teaching them to observe all things
> that I have commanded you; and lo, I am with you
> always, even to the end of the age (Matt. 28:19–20).

Jesus' instruction that the church teach all nations "to the end of the age... *all things* that I have commanded you" is strangely ignored. This self-explanatory message declares that Jesus expected the end-time church to believe, preach and do the same grace works He required of the first-century church. He made no suggestion of a future day with changed doctrine and lessened power. Faith in Him and obedience to the Word would be the deciding factor for the church's success or failure. This was true even with the original apostles; their failures were due to "unbelief" (Matt. 17:20). So also with us. Gifts of the Spirit have not been withdrawn; it is the church's belief in them that has perished. The authority of Jesus' words remain unchanged: "Observe... all things... to the end of the age." It takes great effort to deny the obvious intent of that statement.

Key Point:

In today's church, grace has been reduced to a theology about future life and stripped of its gifts in this life.

In the modern pulpit, grace saves the soul but will not heal the body. That is a contradiction of the meaning of *charis*. Were that true, there would be no resurrection for physical man. The issue is settled. We have no choice but to preach the full New Testament message exactly as it is. Where religious doctrine conflicts with the Word, we are compelled to stand with the Author of the Word. Consider these statistics:

American missions statistician, David Barrett, reports that approximately 33 percent of the world's people are Christians, at least in name. According to Barrett, church members total 1.898 billion, and 1.3 billion attend services. And significantly, pentecostal/charismatic Christianity is growing fastest![1]

More than 70 percent of the progress in world evangelism from the time of Christ until today has occurred since 1900. Seventy percent of that progress happened since the end of World War II; 70 percent of that growth occurred in a 36-month period.[2]

In Latin America, for example, believers are getting saved at four times their population growth rate. Eighty percent of that increase results from those preaching the New Testament work of the Holy Spirit.[3]

John Wesley said it well: "Give me one hundred preachers who fear nothing but sin, and desire nothing but God, and I care not a straw whether they be clergymen or laymen; such alone will shake the gates of hell and set up the kingdom of heaven on earth. God does nothing but in answer to prayer."[4]

My question to you is this: Do you sincerely want to experience everything Jesus provided for you? Are you willing to trust the Holy Spirit to do His full work in your life? Will you get out of the Father's way, surrender control to Him and not interfere with His plan? If so, He will work through you, and everyone will be blessed. How can we know that? He said so!

Obedience to Christ

Believers are in the same circumstance as soldiers on the battlefield: Both must obey textbook instructions as well as orders from the commanding officer. Soldiers who have been taught how to use their weapons do not do so until they are told. Identically, we are to obey our commanding officer, the Holy Spirit, and not to exercise our spiritual gifts merely because the New Testament tells us how. Such an attitude is presumption, not faith; it produces frustration and failure. Be aware of this additional caution: God has "made us sufficient as ministers of the new covenant, not of the letter but of the Spirit; for the letter kills, but the Spirit gives life" (2 Cor. 3:6). Many Christians are shocked to realize that the "letter" of the New Testament, when preached apart from the Spirit's anointing, produces deathly, spiritless religion. Grace-destroying legalism and fatal doctrinalizing today is a direct result of such preaching.

Churches forget that Jesus was speaking to them, not sinners, when He said, "Behold, I stand at the door and knock." Not only so, but He also warned the church, "I will come to you quickly and remove your lampstand from its place—unless you repent" (Rev. 2:5). That warning rests upon one primary fact: The church having left its "first love" (Rev. 2:4). Nowhere does this departure from the church's first love reveal itself more than in her denial of the "blood of sprinkling."

Let me explain: In Moses' day, the Old Testament was sanctified by the sprinkling of animal blood. (See Hebrews 9:19.) That act eternally authenticated it. That being so, how much more was the New Testament sealed by the sprinkling of the blood of the Messiah? (See Hebrews 12:24.) Christians would treat the authenticity of the New Testament with much more fear and trembling if they understood the magnitude of their abuse: "Of how much worse punishment, do you suppose, will he be thought worthy who has trampled the Son of God underfoot, counted the blood of the covenant by which he was sanctified a common thing, and insulted the Spirit of grace?" (Heb. 10:29).

The Battle Against Spiritual Gifts

Two major claims are made against the validity of spiritual gifts. First, they claim all miraculous gifts vanished with the death of the apostle John in A.D. 96. This is based in part on Paul's statement, "Truly the signs of an apostle were accomplished among you with all perseverance, in signs and wonders and mighty deeds" (2 Cor. 12:12). The assumption is made that "signs, wonders, mighty deeds" were to verify the authenticity of the original twelve, plus Paul, and then terminated with their deaths.

Second, it is said that the miraculous works of the Spirit were withdrawn when the New Testament canon was complete. That argument is based on this verse: "Love never fails. But whether there are prophecies, they will fail; whether there are tongues, they will cease; whether there is knowledge, it will vanish away. For we know in part and we prophesy in part. But when that which is perfect has come, then that which is in part will

119

be done away" (1 Cor. 13:8–10).

The argument contends "that which is perfect" refers to the completed text of the New Testament. When the last authorized writing was finished in the year A.D. 90 (so the claim goes), prophecy, tongues and knowledge were withdrawn. That meant that parts of Paul's first letter to the Corinthians were only valid for approximately thirty years. Canonizing of New Testament books (determining which ones were authentic and to be included in Scripture), was not done until the year A.D. 367. By that time, Christianity had spread to Northern Europe and the Far East with no way for those remote areas to know the Scripture had been changed. So, Paul's obsolete teachings were left in the Bible without any explanation of their irrelevance.

If "that which is perfect" refers to New Testament Scripture, then we have a major challenge to the perfection of the Bible. It causes the following statements to no longer be true.

1. Paul's First Corinthian letter was perfect. (By the way, all who believe in the inspiration of Scripture agree with this statement.)
2. The New Testament when completed was perfect.

If 1 Corinthians 12 and 14 became outdated and invalid when the Bible was completed, then the long-awaited "perfect" book was not perfect at all. Canonization only destroyed its perfection. Who can sincerely believe this? The idea is absurd. It defies logic. Paul himself terminated such an argument when he wrote Timothy: "*All* Scripture is given by inspiration of God, and is profitable for doctrine, for reproof, for correction, for instruction in righteousness, that the man of God may be complete, thoroughly equipped for every good work" (2 Tim. 3:16–17, emphasis added).

We need to understand what Paul is *really* referring to when he speaks of "that which is perfect." The key is the word *then*. Observe its three usages in the text: "But when that which is perfect has come, *then* that which is in part will be done away... For now we see in a mirror, dimly, but *then* face to face. Now I know in part, but *then* I shall know just as I also am known" (1 Cor. 13:10, 12, emphasis added). All three times the word *then* appears, it points to the same future perfection.

Honesty forces us to face these questions: Have we come to the time when we no longer "see in a mirror, dimly, but face to face?" No. Have we come to the time when we no longer know "in part" but "as I also am known?" No. Then have we come to the time when "that which is perfect has come?" Obviously the answer is no.

When does this future perfection take place? To my satisfaction, the answer is given with the use of another "then." It is this: "When the Son of Man comes in His glory... *then* the King will say to those on His right hand, 'Come, you blessed of My Father, inherit the kingdom prepared for you from the foundation of the world'" (Matt. 25:31, 34, emphasis added).

Paul exhorted the Corinthians to "come short in no gift [*charisma*], eagerly waiting for the revelation of our Lord Jesus Christ" (1 Cor. 1:7). The duration of spiritual gifts is the same length as the church's waiting for the Lord's return. Regarding the unbroken continuation of miraculous ministry, Jesus specifically said,

> Go therefore and make disciples of all the nations,... teaching them to observe all things that I have commanded you; and lo, I am with you always, even to the end of the age (Matt. 28:19–20).

Hear His words carefully: "Make disciples of all

nations... teaching [all nations to the end of the age] to observe *all things* that I have commanded you." We cannot deny the obvious message of His words.

But that is not all. He further said,

> These signs will follow those who believe: In My name they will cast out demons; they will speak with new tongues; they will take up serpents; and if they drink anything deadly, it will by no means hurt them; they will lay hands on the sick, and they will recover (Mark 16:17–18).

Jesus said that miraculous signs would follow "those who *believe*." Peter's sermon on the Day of Pentecost supports this view. He said:

> It shall come to pass in the last days, says God, That I will pour out of My Spirit on all flesh; Your sons and your daughters shall prophesy, your young men shall see visions, your old men shall dream dreams. And on My menservants and on My maidservants I will pour out My Spirit in those days; And they shall prophesy. I will show wonders in heaven above and signs in the earth beneath... (Acts 2:17–19).

There is no reference in these passages to miracles being limited to the original apostles. We can either believe Jesus or the modern critics. We cannot believe both.

Be aware: it is not the doctrine of miracles which is under attack; it is the doctrine of *grace*. The argument against spiritual gifts is far too inadequate to invalidate a Bible doctrine as significant as the subject of grace.

Bible writers were not ambiguous and vague about their message. Quite the opposite—they were direct, unapologetic, bold about the absolute reliability of God's Word.

Spiritual Gifts in Early Church History

Those who argue that the Holy Spirit's power ended with the death of the first apostles are merely ignorant of their own church history. For example,

1. **Ignatius** (A.D. 33–110) was the third pastor at Antioch, and his ministry paralleled the apostles'. He exercised the gift of prophecy and relied upon its operation in the church into the second century.

2. **Justin Martyr** (A.D. 100–165) wrote that Christians in his day possessed miraculous "gifts of the Spirit of God."

3. **Irenaeus** (A.D. 130–200), who was Bishop of Lyons, France, said, "We have heard of many of the brethren who have foreknowledge of the future, visions and prophetic utterances; others, by laying on of hands, heal the sick and restore them to health... We hear of many members of the church who have prophetic gifts, and, by the Spirit speak with all kinds of tongues, and bring men's secret thoughts to light for their own good, and expound the mysteries of God." Irenaeus also spoke of people being raised from the dead. He insisted that these gifts were not restricted to a local congregation but were present throughout the universal church.

4. **Tertullian** (A.D. 160–225) the greatest theologian of his day, in instructing new believers about their receiving the charismatic gifts of the Holy Spirit, said that they should rise from the waters of baptism, praying and expecting the gifts of the Spirit to come upon them.

5. **Eusebius** (A.D. 260–340), the most recognized early Christian historian, wrote of believers exercising all the spiritual gifts. Words of wisdom, knowledge, faith, healings, tongues and numerous miracles were commonplace among them.

6. **Cyril** (A.D. 315–387), Bishop of Jerusalem, gave instructions to new Christians to expect in baptism the same miraculous gifts as the first apostles. "If you believe," he wrote, "you will receive not just remission of sins, but also do things which pass man's power. And may you be worthy of the gift of prophecy also! ... Prepare yourselves for the reception of the heavenly gifts."

7. **Augustine** (A.D. 354–430), the great pastor-bishop and writer, in his early ministry denied miraculous gifts but was forced to acknowledged his error when some seventy extraordinary healings occurred in his congregations. At the time of his writing, Christians still cast out demons and experienced "falling under the power of the Spirit."[5]

Reliability of the Oldest Biblical Manuscripts

The most common attack against Scripture centers upon the reliability of ancient manuscripts and their having been copied numerous times. Since we have only copies and not the original works of the apostolic writers, how can we intelligently defend a book that is thousands of years old? Our defense of the Bible academically can begin with this observation: There are *no original copies* of any of the following ancient manuscripts. For example,

1. **Plato:** Greek philosopher. His writings are found in a mere *seven* manuscripts, the oldest copy written *twelve hundred* years after his death.

2. **Aristotle:** Greek philosopher, student of Plato, tutor of Alexander the Great. Only *five* copies of any one work of Aristotle exist, and none of these were written less than *fourteen hundred* years after his death.

3. **Herodotus:** Greek historian. Only *eight* manuscripts

survive; these were copied *thirteen hundred* years after the original.

4. **Euripides:** Greek playwright. *Nine* manuscripts exist, dated *thirteen hundred* years after they were first written.[6]

One is immediately struck by the scarcity of copies of these authors and the vast time lapse between the originals and today's reproductions. Yet no one questions their authenticity. Contrast the scarcity of works done by these secular writers to the abundance of New Testament copies. Reknown scholar and professor, Dr. F. F. Bruce, verified approximately four thousand ancient Greek New Testament manuscripts still in existence.[7] Two complete manuscripts are dated less than three hundred years after the original. Most of the New Testament is preserved in copies written less than two hundred years after Jesus. Some existing books were composed about *one hundred* years after the originals. Part of one book came *within a generation* of the first-century.[8]

If approximately four thousand ancient New Testament manuscripts survived the ravages of time, we are overwhelmed with this question: How large was the original number of others, now lost, that exploded upon the public in the first centuries? What was the motivation—the power—that excited early believers into mass production of this book? The answer, of course, is that the book itself was composed by the Holy Spirit and contained His miraculous anointing. Those who read it became motivated to copy and preserve it. The Bible's claim to authenticity is totally beyond the reach of all other writers of antiquity. As believers, we stand secure in its reliability.

Two of the ancient manuscripts, the Sinaitic and Vatican, do not contain the last eleven verses that appear in the King James Version of Mark's Gospel. These verses do appear in other ancient manuscripts and were quoted by Irenaeus and Hippolytus in the second century. The controversy involves not just the antiquity of the passage but also the contents. It says this:

> These signs will follow those who believe: In My name they will cast out demons; they will speak with new tongues; they will take up serpents; and if they drink anything deadly, it will by no means hurt them; they will lay hands on the sick, and they will recover (Mark 16:17–18).

A major complaint regards the statement: "They shall take up serpents." This passage has had two adverse effects: At the suggestion of handling snakes, some have rejected the passage altogether. Others, having determined to prove the passage literally, have suffered snakebite and died. Neither position is valid. The Greek verb *airo*, translated as "take up," means "to seize, bear away, cast out" in the sense of removing violently. The same word is used in John the Baptist's introduction of Jesus, "Behold! The Lamb of God who *takes away* the sin of the world!" (John 1:29). Jesus never caressed or fondled sin; He snatched it away in angered fury. The expression, "They will take up serpents" is parallel to one Jesus made earlier, "I give you the authority to trample on serpents..." (Luke 10:19). In both instances, trampling and snatching away, serpents are parabolic examples of demonic power; power that is under the authority of Spirit-filled believers.

Chapter Eight

God's Five-Fold Ministry and Satan's Five-Fold Opposition

It cannot be coincidental that the five-fold ministry of the New Testament is paralleled by a five-fold satanic opposition. Nor is it by chance that the same five-fold pattern existed between ancient Israel and her enemies. This similarity of warfare in the Old and New Testaments mandates the church's learning from the success and failure of God's ancient people. The apostle Paul identified Jesus' five-fold ministry to the church in this way:

And He Himself gave some to be
  1. apostles, some
  2. prophets, some
  3. evangelists, and some
  4. pastors and
  5. teachers,

for the equipping of the saints for the work of ministry, for the edifying of the body of Christ, till we all come to the unity of the faith and of the knowledge of the Son of God, to a perfect man, to the measure of the

127

stature of the fullness of Christ (Eph. 4:11–13).

The apostle then went on to identify Satan's five-fold opposition:

Put on the whole armor of God, that you may be able to stand against the wiles of the
1. devil. For we do not wrestle against flesh and blood, but against
2. principalities, against
3. powers, against the
4. rulers of the darkness of this age, against
5. spiritual hosts of wickedness in the heavenly places (Eph. 6:11–12).

Observe that this same five-fold pattern existed between the Old Testament saints and their enemies:

1. Abraham fought five kings in the Valley of Siddim. (See Genesis 14:8.)
2. Moses warred with the five kings of Midian. (See Numbers 31:8.)
3. Israel battled the five kings of the Amalakites. (See Exodus 17:9; Genesis 14:7–8.)
4. Joshua killed the five kings of the Amorites. (See Joshua 10:16–26.)
5. Israel was vexed by the five lords of the Philistines. (See Joshua 13:3.)
6. Israel was constantly threatened by the five capital cities of Philistia: Ashdod, Gath, Ekron, Ashkelon, Gaza. (See 1 Samuel 6.)
7. David chose five stones for his battle with Goliath and his four brothers. I Samuel 17:40.
8. God gave Israel a five-priest foundation: Aaron and his four sons. (See Exodus 28:1; Leviticus 8.)
9. Joseph had five of his brothers stand prophetically

before Pharaoh, king of Egypt. (See Genesis 47:2.)

The similarity between the Old and New Testament is too accurately fixed for us to ignore its implication. I do not wish to mysticize the number five or to exaggerate its significance. Rather, I desire to point out the reality of the model's existence in Scripture and that its occurrence is totally beyond the realm of chance. Most importantly of all, I wish to aid the church in her spiritual warfare by disclosing as many of the enemy's battle plans as possible. I am not suggesting that each of these five is pitted only against the corresponding number in the other. Not at all. This is open war. In both camps, all oppose all others.

An example of the five-fold opposition is Islam—the greatest earthly foe Israel and the church have ever faced. Again, it cannot be coincidental that the Muslim religion stands upon five pillars, makes five daily proclamations, requires five daily prayers to Mecca and claims five prophets. My purpose in sharing this information is not to malign Muslim people. Jesus died for them equally as for us. He loves Islamic nations, and so must we. My motive is to expose Satan's plan to exploit such innocent ones in advancing his own cause. By uncovering his work, Christians and Muslims alike are benefited and blessed. Violence will end only when the devil's work has been laid bare and stopped.

The Meaning of the Demonic Star

The pentagram, or demonic star, which is used universally in various forms of Satanism, has five points. Observe this: Two points are always upward, one downward, two extend sideways. The symbol creates the face of a goat devil—horns, ears, beard. Horns speak of authority; ears of hearing and knowledge; the beard represents age and wisdom. God's assignment to the five-fold ministry is to destroy all of them. How is that done? This Scripture tells us:

> Finally, my brethren, be strong in the Lord and in the power of His might... Take up the whole armor of God, that you may be able to withstand in the evil day, and having done all, to stand. Stand therefore, having girded your waist with truth, having put on the breastplate of righteousness, and having shod your feet with the preparation of the gospel of peace; above all, taking the shield of faith with which you will be able to quench all the fiery darts of the wicked one. And take the helmet of salvation, and the sword of the Spirit, which is the word of God; praying always with all prayer and supplication in the Spirit, being watchful to this end with all perseverance and supplication for all the saints (Eph. 6:10, 13–18).

Satan's ancient war is not against creation but against the Creator. He wants the universe for his own, but as he is unable to obtain it, he then seeks its destruction. You and I are not his primary targets. Since we are designed "in the image and likeness" of God and are objects of His love and heirs of His glory, we are the secondary objects of Satan's attack. He would easily obliterate us were it not that Christ voluntarily took human form and made Himself vulnerable in our behalf.

Prior to the incarnation, Jesus was totally beyond the reach of the prince of darkness. In exposing Himself on Satan's earthly realm and proving His superiority in every aspect, He "disarmed principalities and powers, He made a public spectacle of them, triumphing over them in it" (Col. 2:15).

It is vital we understand the five-fold ministry is empowered through a *personal extension of Jesus Himself.* "Christ in you, the hope of glory" (Col. 1:27) brings success in ministry. It is not human ability. Ministers who do not recognize this holy truth and try to accomplish the work in their own strength will ultimately fail—or substitute their soulish imitation for God's success. Examine these scriptures that speak about Jesus' relationship to the five-fold ministry:

1. He is Apostle: "Therefore, holy brethren, partakers of the heavenly calling, consider the *Apostle and High Priest* of our confession, Christ Jesus" (Heb. 3:1, italics added).

2. He is Prophet: "For Moses truly said to the fathers, 'The LORD your God will raise up for you a *Prophet* like me from your brethren. Him you shall hear in all things, whatever He says to you'" (Acts 3:22, italics added).

3. He is Evangelist: "He went into the synagogue on the Sabbath day, and stood up to read... 'The Spirit of the LORD is upon Me, because He has anointed Me to *preach* the gospel to the poor...'" (Luke 4:16–22, italics added).

4. He is Pastor: "I am the good *shepherd* [pastor]. The good shepherd gives His life for the sheep" (John 10:11, italics added).

5. He is Teacher: "Nicodemus... came to Jesus by night and said to Him, 'Rabbi, we know that You are a *teacher* come from God...'" (John 3:1–2).

Jesus is the light source for every aspect of the five-fold ministry. Not only so, but the new covenant's apostleship and the old covenant's high priesthood find completion in Him; Jesus wears the double crown. Absolute, unconditional, eternal authority flows from His having united these two offices. "In Him dwells all the fullness of the

Godhead bodily; and you are complete in Him, who is the head of *all* principality and power" (Col. 2:9). He united both Old and New Testament functions so that we might share in the exercise of His authority.

In the Book of Revelation, Jesus wears two crowns: the *diadema* (See Revelation 19:12.) and the *stephanos*. (See Revelation 6:2.) The *diadem* was made of gold and could be gained only by royal birth. As the Son of God, Jesus is heir to the throne of heaven. As David's royal offspring, He is the lion of the tribe of Judah. The second crown, the *stephanos*, made of ivy, oak leaves, violets and other flowers, could be worn only by the victor. This crown was awarded to winners in the Greek games. Only the champion could wear it. As the one who triumphed over Satan, Jesus also wears this crown. Being heir of both covenants—apostleship and high priesthood—and *both being conquerors of powers of darkness*, Jesus wears dual crowns.

As Apostle, Jesus is the voice of God downward to the people. As High Priest, He is the voice of the people upward to God. Apostolically, Jesus speaks to the church through Scripture and the Holy Spirit. As High Priest at the throne of heaven, He speaks to the Father on behalf of the church. (See Hebrews 3:1.) Jesus is both origin and termination of these offices: each springs from Him; each concludes in Him. He is Alpha and Omega—the Beginning and the End. Not only is He the fulfillment of the Aaronic priesthood, but He has also been made "High Priest forever according to the order of Melchizedek" (Heb. 6:20.) This dual-priesthood enthrones Him forever as Intercessor.

Are There Apostles Today?

As I understand Scripture, apostleship falls into two categories: First, there are the "twelve apostles of the Lamb" whose names are written in the foundation of the Holy

City. (See Revelation 21:14.) This number is fixed, inalterable, and will never be exceeded. The qualification for these men was that each had been a "witness of Jesus' resurrection" (Acts 1:22).

Second, in the Greek Scripture where the word *apostolos* appears more frequently than in English translations, it means "sent ones," "delegates," "ambassadors" or "messengers." Let me give scriptural examples:

"If anyone inquires about Titus... or if our brethren are inquired about, they are messengers [*apostolos*] of the churches..." (2 Cor. 8:23).

"Yet I considered it necessary to send to you Epaphroditus... but your messenger [*apostolos*]" (Phil. 2:25).

Barnabas is also called an apostle: "But when the apostles Barnabas and Paul heard this, they tore their clothes..." (Acts 14:14).

These men are not equal with the "apostles of the Lamb" but in a lessor way are legitimate bearers of this title.

In Paul's first Thessalonian letter he begins with the names "Paul, Silvanus, and Timothy" and then proceeds to use the personal pronouns "we," "our" and "us" some twenty times. Count them. In 1 Thessalonians 2:6 he says: "Nor did we seek glory from men, either from you or from others, when we might have made demands as apostles of Christ." Notice the letter "s." The word *apostles* is plural, not singular. What is Paul saying? He is acknowledging that Silvanus and Timothy were apostles with him. Were they his equal? No. Their ministries never achieved what his did. Even so, Scripture acknowledges them as "sent ones" in a valid sense. To deny their apostleship would be a flagrant denial of Bible fact.

In Acts 1, Matthias was chosen to replace Judas Iscariot. That restored the number twelve—but that was only the first of the changes to the twelve. We later find that King Herod killed the apostle James, Acts 12:1–2, and another James, "the Lord's brother," was added to the twelve. Paul makes specific reference to seeing this apostle during his visit to Jerusalem. (See Galatians 1:19.) It was this new James who presided over the Council of Jerusalem. (See Acts 15:13.) Approximately twenty-five apostles are identified in the New Testament.

To me, the most significant proof that the five-fold ministry of apostles, prophets, evangelists, pastors and teachers is still with us, is verified by the Ephesian letter. We learned in the Gospels that the original apostles were given *before* the Resurrection and were witnesses of it. Ephesians tells us that Jesus gave other apostles *after* the Resurrection. Paul explains, *"When He ascended on high,* He led captivity captive, and gave gifts to men... And He Himself gave some to be apostles..."* (Eph. 4:8, 11, emphasis added). Study this judiciously: "When He ascended on high [*after the Resurrection*]... He Himself gave some to be apostles." These apostles came later than the original twelve.

In the Book of Revelation, Jesus commended the church at Ephesus because it "tested those who say they are apostles and are not, and have found them liars" (2:2). Why would the church have tested anyone if there were only the twelve? On the contrary, believers had to examine those claiming apostleship because the gift was still present and functioning. The church in our day must heed this same admonition: Everyone claiming ministry in the body of Christ, whether apostle or pastor, must be put to the test of Scripture. Beware those who are prideful, arrogant, self-serving, controlling. "Follow after that which is good." Remember, "Many false prophets have gone out into the world" (1 John 4:1).

What proof do we seek in those recognized as apostles?

Paul answers that question. Of himself, he said to the Corinthians, "The signs of an apostle were accomplished among you with all perseverance, in signs and wonders and mighty deeds... I myself was not burdensome to you." (2 Cor. 12:12–13). Observe that Paul identifies two character traits: "perseverance" (patience) and his not being "burdensome" to the saints. In addition, he lists three action words: "signs, wonders, and mighty deeds." In varying degrees, these qualities must be present in those claiming apostleship today.

Let me also answer another question: In what capacity were the apostles of the Lamb infallible? Peter tells us that "Holy men of God *spoke* as they were moved by the Holy Spirit" (2 Pet. 1:20–21, emphasis added.) As the Holy Spirit articulated through them, they wrote correctly. He dictated; they transcribed. He inspired; they recorded. Jesus had earlier promised them, "The Holy Spirit, whom the Father will send in My name, He will teach you all things, and bring to your remembrance all things that I said to you" (John 14:26). The writing of Scripture was not trusted to men's fallible memory but to the perfect revelation of God. Of Himself, Jesus declared, "My doctrine is not Mine, but His who sent Me" (John 7:16).

The Bible teaches apostolic infallibility only in regard to the writing of Scripture. There is no such claim for the apostles' private lives, personal faith, indestructible health, etc. It is important that we understand this. Without this knowledge, we will needlessly try to force Scripture into positions that are unrealistic and wrong. The apostles and prophets were men "with a nature like ours" (James 5:17). Not only were they subject to fail but frequently did so. Paul rebuked Peter to his face because of his inconsistencies regarding the Jews. (See Galatians 2:11.) Trophimus was left at Miletus sick. (see 2 Timothy

4:20.) Paul and Barnabas's quarrel ended their joint ministry. (See Acts 15:36–41.) Timothy endured "often infirmities" (1 Tim. 5:23). At one point Paul "despaired even of life" (2 Cor. 1:8). Was it his personal faith that triumphed in crisis? No, the weakness of his faith brought despair. Instead, God's grace was his sole rescuer.

Paul apparently suffered eye disease at one point in his ministry. (See Galatians 4:13–15.) The Galatian letter, which he identifies as having been written with his "own hand" in "large letters," also speaks of the people's willingness to "pluck out their eyes" for him. To the Corinthians he confessed that his "bodily presence is weak" (2 Cor. 10:10). These were not discouragements. He later explained, "I... boast in my infirmities, that the power of Christ may rest upon me" (2 Cor. 12:7–10).

In view of this should we assume that Paul, Peter, Timothy, Barnabas and the others were free of failure, sin and disease? Not at all. Rather, we are to rejoice that God used these men in spite of their weakness. Identically, our failures do not keep us from sharing in Paul's testimony: "Out of them all the Lord delivered me" (2 Tim. 3:11). Simply stated, we must realize that these men were not angelic beings, living in glorified bodies, immune to frustration and failure. Each was subject to the same consequence of humanity as we are today. The Holy Spirit worked His perfect will through imperfect men. The glory therefore goes to Him, not them. They triumphed over their adversities—so may we! Hallelujah!

Are there apostles today? Yes. These are "sent ones." They did not volunteer for ministry but were *called*. Like Paul, many struggled with that divine summons. Some fought it. But "[God's] hand is stretched out, and who will turn it back?" (Isa. 14:26–27). Are these men infallible? Not at all! But they are aflame with holy love for Christ and His bride. Do they promote themselves? No. They are concerned with truth, not titles. They seek God, not gold; purity, not praise. Pray for these men! Support them! From the others, turn away.

The Destruction of High Places

In the Old Testament, we read of godly kings destroying the "high places" (2 Kin. 18:4); and in the New Testament, the saints "pulling down [spiritual] strongholds" (2 Cor. 10:4). High places were pagan sites of worship; these were visible, physical places on hilltops where sacrifices were made to heathen gods. Strongholds are invisible, powerful spiritual sites of demonic activity in the heavens. Both are elevated places.

In each case, the kingdom of God is not sufficiently established in the ruins of Satan's domain until the altar of God has been rebuilt in that place. (See 1 Kings 18:30.) This means that a person absolutely must refill a former pagan life with the power of Jesus Christ. Cleansing the pagan site is incomplete until the altar of God has been restored. The first without the second is both ineffective and dangerous.

We must be "more than conquerors." Merely capturing and subduing the enemy is not enough. The powers of evil and darkness must be replaced with the powers of holiness and light. Part of the church's astonishing role in this warfare is that "the manifold wisdom of God might be made known... to the principalities and powers in the heavenly places" (Eph. 3:10).

In the whole of Scripture there is probably no more astounding job description of the church than this one. The body of believers is God's instrument for proclaiming His victory to the demonic powers surrounding the earth. Significantly, Jesus made His corresponding proclamation in Hades, or lower world. (See 1 Peter 3:19.) He has given the privilege to us to make the announcement in the heavenlies, or upper world. Both dimensions are shaken by that proclamation.

Why did God choose to project "wisdom" into the demonic region? Why not His omnipotence, sovereignty or other character trait? Second, why did He choose the church for that projection? Paul answered the first question when he said, "We preach Christ crucified... Christ the power of God and the *wisdom* of God" (1 Cor. 1:23–24, emphasis added). It is not wisdom in its ordinary sense that shatters the prince of the power of the air. Rather, it is wisdom personified as Christ. (See Proverbs 8:12, 22–31.) The saints' proclamation of Christ as the wisdom and Word of God brings desolation to powers of darkness. Since Satan caused man's fall, God wills that man, empowered with the Holy Spirit, cause Satan's fall. Even Satan will reap what he has sown. (See Galatians 6:7.)

The conclusion is unavoidable: God intends that the five-fold ministry, *undergirded by the rest of the church* and acting corporately as one complete body, decimate the prince of darkness. This can only be done when the church truly discovers that it is "complete in Him, who is the head of all principality and power" (Col. 2:10). Jesus confirmed this when He said: "I give you the authority to trample on serpents and scorpions, and over *all* the power of the enemy, and nothing shall by any means hurt you" (Luke 10:19). Regarding the church, it is the purpose of God that "the gates of Hades shall not prevail against it" (Matt. 16:18). This can be accomplished only "according to the power that works in us" (Eph. 3:20).

We have an identical parallel in the Old Testament's message through Moses: "Therefore understand today that the LORD your God is He who goes over before you as a consuming fire. He will destroy [*shaw-mad*] them and bring them down before you; so you shall drive them out and destroy [*aw-bad*] them quickly, as the LORD has said to you" (Deut. 9:3).

It is important that we understand the difference between God and Israel's destroying the enemy. Two different Hebrew words are used.

shaw-mad: "to desolate utterly"
aw-bad: "to break, destroy, be rid of"[1]

In *shaw-mad*, God utterly crushes the enemy. In *aw-bad*, Israel was to "clear the field" of their presence. Identically, Jesus utterly demolished the power of Satan and his hosts; the task of the church is to drive Satan and his hosts from our presence.

David's encounter with Goliath provides the most perfect portrayal of conflict between the two kingdoms and the five-fold powers of each. David faced his enemy with five smooth stones—one each for Goliath and his four brothers. The stones symbolized the authority of the original five-fold priesthood of Israel, Aaron and his four sons, and the future five-fold ministry of the church. The number five not only corresponded exactly to the enemy's sum total on the field but was more than sufficient to bring each down. David needed only one stone for Goliath. The other four stones were prophetic, each symbolically containing the names of Goliath's four brothers.

Goliath's call is: "Come to me, and I will give your flesh to the birds of the air and the beasts of the field!" (1 Sam. 17:44).

Jesus' call to mankind is, "Come to Me,… and I will give you rest. Take My yoke upon you and learn from Me,… and you shall find rest for your souls… For My yoke is easy and my burden is light" (Matt. 11:28–30).

Goliath represented the five lords of the Philistines and the five capital cities over which they ruled. The challenge he gave every morning and evening probably occurred when the "morning and evening sacrifices" were taking place in Jerusalem. This was an occult attempt to resist the power being released at the great altar.

David symbolizes Christ who brought Satan to crashing defeat. Jesus said to His disciples, "I give you authority to trample on serpents and scorpions and over all the power of the enemy..." (Luke 10:19). Identically, as David's mighty men brought the other four giants to the earth, so the empowered church, must bring "powers, principalities, rulers of the darkness of this age, spiritual hosts of wickedness in heavenly places," to the ground (Rev. 12:7–12). Remember, Paul said the role of the church in this war is to make known "the manifold wisdom of God..." to the "principalities and powers in heavenly places" (Eph. 3:10).

The Church's Power to Launch Attack

Powers of darkness are penetrated by the church by a trinitarian attack.

> They overcame him [Satan] by the (1) blood of the Lamb and by the (2) word of their testimony, and they (3) did not love their lives to the death (Rev.12:11, numbers added).

In the Great Commission, Jesus said,

> All authority has been given to Me in heaven and on earth. Go... make disciples of all the nations... teaching them to observe *all things* that I have commanded you; and lo, I am with you always, even to the end of the age (Matt. 28:18–20).

The expression "all things" is self-explanatory. Jesus

expected the church in the last age to believe, preach and do the same works which He required of the first-century church. Scripturally, there is no such thing as an "apostolic" and "post-apostolic" church. There is simply "one Lord, one faith, one baptism"—one body of Christ. It is God's purpose that the end-times church be an exact duplicate of the church at Pentecost. Jesus expressed that power, in part, through the five-fold ministry.

Regardless of which part of the five-fold ministries one occupies, the success of his spiritual warfare is absolutely dependent on fulfilling these three stipulations in Revelation 12:11. There is much religious activity that fails because it lacks one or more of these essential requirements. This "threefold cord is not quickly broken" (Eccles. 4:12). It was this same truth identified by David when he told Goliath,

> You come to me with a (1) sword, with a (2) spear, and with a (3) javelin [a carnal trinity]. But I come to you in the name of the LORD of hosts [Father, Son, Holy Spirit—eternal trinity] the God of the armies of Israel, whom you have defied. This day the LORD will deliver you into my hand, and I will strike you and take your head from you... that all the earth may know that there is a God in Israel. Then all this assembly shall know that the LORD does not save with sword and spear; for the battle is the LORD's, and He will give you into our hands" (1 Sam. 17:45–47, numbers added).

David's "taking the head" from Goliath, champion of the giants, was prophetic of Jesus' taking headship from Satan and exposing the powers of his kingdom to spoilage. Like David, Jesus' "mighty men" are capable of "cleaning the field."

The protest is made that today's apostles, prophets,

evangelists, pastors and teachers are no match for Satan's enormous spiritual power. I agree. For that reason Jesus conferred specific authority upon these ministries when He said, "You shall receive power when the Holy Spirit has come upon you" (Acts 1:8). Many in today's church are unaware that this power exists for them. Others are unaware that the power goes far beyond preaching, healing the sick, casting out demons or other localized works.

Specifically, through Christ we are "to stand against the wiles of the devil" and successfully to "wrestle with powers, principalities, rulers, spiritual wickedness." The ones we battle are in the "heavenly places." The word *heavenly* identifies their location, not their character. For that reason, God has "made us sit together in the heavenly places *in* Christ Jesus" (Eph. 2:6). This position does more than give us mere rival authority; it bestows God-assigned victorious power. Nor are we seated there alone; we are *in* Christ, "in Him dwells all the fullness of the Godhead bodily" (Col. 2:9). Being "in Christ," we too are eternal beings, called to wage and win war over lessor angelic beings. The battle is spiritual, not physical. Our assurance is, "He who is in you is greater than he who is in the world" (1 John 4:4).

Jesus gave five signs of miraculous power to the church. He said, "These signs will follow those who believe: In My name

1. they will cast out demons;
2. they will speak with new tongues;
3. they will take up serpents;
4. and if they drink anything deadly, it will by no means hurt them;
5. they will lay hands on the sick, and they will recover" (Mark 16:17–18, numbers added).

142

When Jesus told the disciples, "You shall be baptized with the Holy Spirit not many days from now... You shall receive power when the Holy Spirit has come upon you" (Acts 1:5,8), He was explaining that their source of power would be the same as His. He had received the anointing of the Holy Spirit in the Jordan; they would receive the same anointing in the Upper Room. Prior to His promise of Pentecost, He told them, "He who believes in Me, the works that I do he will do also; and greater works than these he will do, because I go to My Father" (John 14:12). Their works would not only be done though the same Holy Spirit but would be additionally fortified because He went "to the Father." As High Priest at the Father's right hand, He would make intercession for them. This was a benefit which He Himself did not have. Perhaps that is one reason He could promise they would do "greater works" than He had done.

Additionally, His ministry had been confined to one tiny nation; they would go to the "ends of the earth." He was heard by thousands; they would be heard by billions.

Jesus could fully expect the miraculous works to accompany the five-fold ministry because it would be a continuation of His own ministry through them. Though He would be in heaven and they on earth, they would remain a part of His body as much as Adam's rib, reformed as Eve, remained a part of Adam. Jesus is still Apostle, Prophet, Evangelist, Pastor and Teacher. The "kingdom and the power and the glory" remain His. (See Matthew 6:13.)

Whenever these ministries fulfill their true role today, it is because the power is proceeding directly from Him. The Holy Spirit is the instrument of transference. Apostleship in a man can never be severed from Apostleship in Jesus. If such a breach occurs between the minister and Jesus in any of the five-fold ministries, the work becomes only a human formality and not a divine reality. In that state, the man is immediate prey to the enemy and powerless to resist his attack.

Many fail because they begin their ministry in the Spirit but attempt to fulfill it through the flesh. (See Galatians 3:3.) The mind or soul, wonderful as it is, is vastly inadequate to satisfy the "high calling" or to battle powers of darkness. Today's ministry must be able to say with Paul, "I serve [God] *with my spirit* in the gospel of His Son" (Rom. 1:9, emphasis added). The human spirit, when joined to the Holy Spirit, is not confined to the small area around it. It is capable of receiving ubiquitous knowledge. The soul is very confined.

Much ministry, tragically, rises from soulishness and lacks in true spiritual power. The difference is not always distinguished easily. Soulishness opens one to pride and the works of the flesh. If the minister falls under its influence, regards himself "more highly than he ought" (Rom. 12:3), the gift ceases to be Christ-like. In that state, the ministry loses its true spiritual nature and becomes wholly soulish. It is then possible for it to decline in three steps: "earthly, sensual [soulish], demonic" (James 3:15).

All ministries are obligated to prove their union with Christ. Jesus commended the church at Ephesus because it had "tested those who say they are apostles and are not, and have found them liars" (Rev. 2:2.)

History confirms that the power of the Holy Spirit remained in the church for the first two centuries. Only as unbelief and paganism entered did the power disappear. The replacement of true spirituality by soulishness and unbelief ultimately stripped the church of authority and left it defenseless before the enemy. The idea that God removed His power at the death of the apostles is insupportable from Scripture or history. This theory is merely an attempt to justify the church's failure.

In the same way the earth became the battleground for Israel and her enemies, the earth is identically the battleground for the war between heaven and hell. The Old Testament wars provided a visible stage upon which the "kingdom of God" and the "kingdom of the prince of darkness" fought their battles in actual, physical combat. Through that public dramatization, the Old Testament supplies a detailed, parabolic example of New Testament warfare. The Jewish wars were neither theoretical nor philosophical; they were literal, bloody confrontations between avowed enemies. By contrast, the invisible warfare in which the New Testament believer is engaged is wholly spiritual.

Israel's war chronicles provide the church with a textbook view of spiritual battles. We have an advantage which the ancient Jews did not have—the blow-by-blow example of their combat. Their model is one which the church absolutely must comprehend. Our success or failure depends on how well we learn.

Chapter Nine

Apostasy and Occultism Will Oppose You

In 1974, while pastor of a congregation in Atlanta, I attended sessions of the Georgia legislature and had lunch with several of the senators. In that year's session, something unusual happened. Several young men dressed gaudily in pink and lavender stood up in the gallery above the Senate chamber and interrupted the proceedings to publicly announce that they were homosexuals. Their purpose was to let the Georgia legislature know that their organizations were going to change the laws in their favor. They were quickly booed down and escorted out. The idea was contemptuous. No one believed them, but the proclamation had been made.

Something else significant occurred in 1974. The American Psychiatric Association removed homosexuality from its list of mental disorders. Probably no one connected the two events as being related. Within a few years however, the declaration voiced by homosexuals in the Georgia Senate was heard everywhere. Laws across the nation were suddenly rewritten to appease "gay-rights" demands. The United States president publicly endorsed the homosexual agenda and sought their support. Pentagon officials and the military forces became embroiled by it. Colleges bent to its influence. Numerous religious groups reversed centuries-old positions and gave in. Hollywood gladly shouted its approval. In the 1996 Olympic Games in Atlanta, Cobb County was refused the right to host official activities because it had earlier voted down a gay-rights demand for preferential treatment.

What Is the Significance of 1974?

In 1949 the unchallenged high priestess of the occult world, Alice A. Bailey, died. Thirty years earlier in 1919, when her career as a medium and psychic reader began, Alice accurately foretold the year of her death. Ms. Bailey, who wrote some twenty-four books of instructions to disciples of the New Age, was not an ordinary psychic. Sorcerers around the world acknowledged her as Satan's appointed messenger of the New Age. Alice's guidebooks were dictated to her, she claimed, by a spirit guide, a Tibetan demon called D.K.

By the time of her death, a network of more than five thousand organizations were listed in just two of the many New Age worldwide directories. These included legitimate-sounding industrial organizations, international music groups, highly organized and well-financed homosexual clubs, witchcraft covens, political bodies, religious societies and others. According to Detroit attorney Constance Cumby, who studied Ms. Bailey and her work thoroughly, "It was sheer evil genius" that manifested in Alice's detailed instructions for her disciples.

Alice's voluminous writing spanned three decades of activity in which she instructed her followers to wait twenty-five years from the time of her death before "going public." That year, 1974, they were to "come out of the closet" and make their influence fully known. Millions of Americans who never heard of Alice Bailey were unaware that a fatal point had been reached in American history. At the infamous Woodstock Concert, near that time, America had its first hard look into the drug pit of human depravity. Woodstock officially introduced the New Age as the "Age of Aquarius."

Nowhere was the change more obvious and deliberate than in the movie industry. Family-oriented films suddenly disappeared as occult ones took their place. A virtual flood of demonized themes hit the screens. Children's heroes were no longer the good guys wearing white; they became the foreboding, black-robed warlocks with mystical powers. The movie designed specifically to glamorize the dark world of spiritism to children was Stephen Spielburg's famous *E.T.* The character, E.T. the extraterrestrial, was a straight-out-of-the-pit demon whom children were taught to love and trust. Having met him, they would more willingly accept his real-life counterparts without fear. Toy manufacturers rushed to a frantic promotion of ghouls, monsters, trolls and outerspace fiends. Ignorant parents allowed their children to cuddle these devilish ploys, unaware that their youngsters were victims of deliberate mental abduction.

The unicorn quickly became a prominent New Age symbol that was eagerly accepted by millions as ornaments in their homes. These naive souls did not realize that the unicorn was a New Age essential because of the philosophy accompanying it. Briefly stated, that philosophy says that the unicorn will bring ultimate peace to mankind after it has destroyed the existing world order. Why did the drug culture, homosexual agenda, demon worship and other "society-destroying" forces suddenly burst upon the scene? Alice's books explain.

Who Is the Target?

The home, as an institution of safety and trust, came under fierce attack. Husbands were portrayed as bungling fools; wives as the abused, unfulfilled prey of male chauvinism. Public school courses began teaching that homosexuality and lesbianism are "alternate lifestyles" and a normal expression of sexuality. Government and corporate employees were forced to take courses desensitizing their antihomosexual attitudes or lose their jobs. Hospital personnel were forced to participate in abortions or be fired. Condoms were given to fourth graders with demonstrations on how to properly use them.

Music, television shows, comic books, bestselling hardbacks were suddenly saturated with messages of occultism and hard-core Satanism. Some public advertising asked the question, "Would you like a spell cast on you?" Fortune-tellers became guest stars on talk shows; celebrities gave testimonies of their powers. Even Santa Claus appeared carrying a magic wand and wearing a psychic star in his cap. The attack on Santa changed his smiling, rotund image into a skinny, ragged old man, with a dirty beard and sinister features.

President Reagan was exposed for side-stepping his Washington advisors and allowing his wife to have his official government agenda arranged through a California-based astrologer. Christians and the church came under the most merciless attack of all. As silently as carbon monoxide poisoning, public opinion was anesthetized into non-resistance.

While we may think the present assault by powers of darkness is bad, believe me, it is going to get much, much worse. Scripture forewarns this will happen; current events prove it so. This may surprise you, but many churches will surrender to the New Age. Some will abdicate by going with it; others will submit by not fighting. Statistician George Barna predicts that in the next ten years thousands of American churches will permanently close their doors.

What once repelled society is now being embraced by it. In May 1996, the University of California hosted the Whole Earth Festival, which adopted as its theme "Kiss Chaos." The strange title was meant to express the festival's eagerness for the anarchy it sees coming upon mankind. Those promoting the festival believe that peace can come to earth only after all existing order has been destroyed. Not only do they anticipate anarchy, but they also promote it. Terrifying? The story gets worse. The organizations they say need to be exterminated include the family, church, government, education, business, commercial life, music, medicine—everything that presently holds humanity together. Since civilized society has been totally polluted, everything must go. Christianity, of course, is the major culprit in that polluting.

This hellish concept is the center core of New Age philosophy. In their depraved view, worldwide anarchy is the only instrument that can remove obstacles to their peace; chaos should be welcomed affectionately with a kiss. The idea is demonic insanity at its worst. Most frightening of all, its program is already more successful than we dare realize. Do you need proof? Schoolchildren going berserk and killing teachers, parents and other youngsters is only the forerunner of chaos to come. These killing sprees are not accidental; they are the deadly fruit of a tree purposely planted in our backyard. Depraved rock music urges teenagers to kill their parents and put them out of their suffering. Such hellish influences injected into the minds of impressionable young people, some distorted by drugs, can't be stopped because it violates the right of "free speech," our leaders say. Never mind a child's right to a safe environment.

Anti-God organizations with unlimited legal help defend degeneracy while fighting morality and the church. Don't assume that the chaos idea is merely the passing lunacy of madmen chanting mantras. Not so. It is Satan's long-planned strategy for the end of the age. Like it or not, you and I are a part of the end. The church needs to wake up and get real with the message it preaches. Humanity faces crisis. In the climax, all genuine believers will eagerly accept *everything* the Scripture says about the Holy Spirit. His miraculous works will be received without challenge. Survival will depend on it. Pastors will be forced to decide between allegiance to Christ or their denominations. Church members will be driven into the same decision. The Holy Spirit will then pour His power into that new, truly committed body.

In all of this frightening talk, is there any good news for the church? Absolutely. First of all, Jesus said, "Now when these things begin to happen, look up and lift up your heads, because your redemption draws near" (Luke 21:28). Second, events in the next few years will force Christians to get serious about the Holy Spirit. The decision will be required of everyone. Denominations that now reject the baptism in the Holy Spirit and the operation of His gifts will eagerly accept them—or perish. Vaudevillian Christians and others desiring to "make a good showing in the flesh" (Gal. 6:12), will find themselves stripped of phoniness. Cosmetic religion will be laid bare. The party will be over. "Holy" pride will perish. God will demand reality. Survival will depend on it. Only those individuals and churches empowered by the Holy Spirit will survive. Nominal Christianity will have come to its end.

On the calendar of human history, we probably have only moments left. Our attitude should be, "Even so, come, Lord Jesus!" (Rev. 22:20). In the final hour, some believers will be like the five foolish virgins who were closed out of the marriage feast. (See Matthew 25:1–13.) Don't be among them! Don't make the careless claim, "'We have Abraham as our father!' (Matt. 3:9). We are God's elect!" God will not hear empty talk. He demands fruit, not religious chatter. If you are in grace, prove it! While many are crying in that day, "Lord, Lord, open to us! Open to us!" He will turn away. Instead, He will be focusing His love on the true bride. She will be a Bible believer–not a Bible bluffer. If you are one of those who rejects certain Scriptures because of prejudice, you are on dangerous ground. Such an attitude is deadly. Jesus commended one of the seven churches of Asia by saying, you "have kept My word" (Rev. 3:8). For the unsaved, the anticipation is this:

> But the cowardly, unbelieving, abominable, murderers, sexually immoral, sorcerers, idolaters, and all liars shall have their part in the lake which burns with fire and brimstone, which is the second death" (Rev. 21:8).

If you ever expect to get right with God, do it now! Time is running out. The end will come in a moment, in the twinkling of an eye. (See 1 Corinthians 15:52.) In that day, the New Age will be exposed as the old lie. Be certain that you are among those who are "caught up... to meet the Lord in the air" (1 Thess. 4:17). Do not be deceived! Christ, not Alice, offers grace and redemption. We are living in a time of tremendous blessing and power. Thank God! But be forewarned. Whenever fires of revival begin to burn, insects are always drawn to the light. The gospel had barely touched Samaria when Simon the Sorcerer stepped from the shadows and stood in the way. Paul's ministry in Philippi, the doorway to Europe, had just opened when he was joined by a medium who began endorsing his ministry. Later he was resisted by Alexander the coppersmith, who apparently worked in occult powers. At Ephesus, the resistance against Paul reached its greatest strength. All of these efforts ultimately failed. Simon was exposed and told publicly to repent. The fortune-telling girl had demons exorcised, and she was set totally free. At Ephesus, the riot was followed by revival, and the kingdom of God was firmly planted in the decay of fallen paganism. A huge pile of witchcraft books was publicly burned in the town square. Alexander apparently remained a thorn in Paul's side. In Moses' day, the final attempt to stop Israel from entering the Promised Land was made by the false prophet, Balaam. He too failed and was killed.

Today we are exposed to the same attacks of occultism as was the first-century church. Unlike our Apostolic fathers, unfortunately, we are not as capable in recognizing and resisting them. The Scripture forewarns that in the end times a greater number of seducing spirits will invade the earth. Most of the church is uninformed and ill-prepared for the attack. Spiritualism and spirituality are being blended in such a devious way that some Christians cannot tell the difference.

The primary target of these spiritual foes is the kingdom of God. Their plan is to disrupt, divide, weaken and scatter the church's ranks. That way they undermine every area of Christian life. The spirit which poses the greatest danger to the church is a religious spirit. Undetected, it attempts to join the church and travel with it. This spirit is not denominational; it can as easily be Muslim or Hindu, Pentecostal or Baptist. Disguised in piety and speaking religious language, its aim is to prevent people from discovering the truth of God. Consequently, its damage usually goes undetected until too late.

People in whom it operates rarely recognize its true nature in themselves. It can be in a sweet-looking deacon's wife or a domineering pastor. Both see their motive as best for the church. To some probable degree, every congregation is infected with this spirit. Its presence can best be recognized through the Holy Spirit's gift of discerning of spirits. This "exposure by the Spirit" is what happened during Jesus' visit to the synagogue in Capernaum. A man whose demon had probably never before been challenged suddenly started shouting abuses. (See Mark 1:21–28.)

Do not assume this man was an unshaven derelict whom everyone knew was demonized. He may have been a sophisticated leader in the community. In this case, the demon manifested himself only because *he was threatened by the presence of Jesus.* Even today, demons reveal themselves involuntarily when confronted by anointed believers. This explains a mystery: churches can continue peacefully in a spiritually dead state until the Holy Spirit begins to expose the darkness and hidden sin. Instead of churches getting blessed by the Holy Spirit's presence, all hell may break loose. Sometimes there is a mad scramble to return the church to its former darkness. A demon who is in control of a church or person and becomes exposed will always fight viciously to protect his "house." A religious spirit can quote more Scripture, pray more fervently and preach louder than a legitimate pastor. He will intimidate, ridicule and slander his opponent—usually a God-appointed shepherd—all in the name of religion. Such a demon, working through another vessel, can convince many that his is the legitimate ministry. If intimidation fails, he will resort to accusations about being persecuted.

Some churches have been dominated by these spirits for generations; it is not unusual for them to work through a woman whose husband appears strong before the congregation but is privately weak in her hands. This husband and wife combination reproduces the religious syndrome of Ahab and Jezebel. Few spiritual strategies are more deadly to godly leadership in a church. Though it may be painful to correct, the church has no choice but to treat the situation the same as it would any other occult influence. Here are some danger signals in people operating in seducing spirits:

1. They go from church to church and are usually "lone rangers" who are in submission to no one, have no authentic spiritual covering, and no valid credentials.
2. Their past is one of chaos and strife in other churches.
3. Their super-spirituality is quickly displayed and self-promoting.
4. They are not submitted to the local pastor; nor do they receive correction.
5. They do not hesitate to undermine the pastor in seducing their followers.
6. They usually identify only with a select group in the church.
7. Their followers are quickly shown the spiritual superiority of the new leader over the recognized church ministry.

While everyone is victimized, the most tragic ones are those who are stolen from the flock they loved. These deluded souls have fallen for the oldest trick in Christian history: *deception*. During the fifty years of my ministry, I have seen it happen repeatedly. Jesus called these church invaders "ravenous wolves" (Matt. 7:15); Paul called them "savage wolves" (Acts 20:29). Nationwide, the church can be forewarned. There are battalions of them on the prowl. More are to come. The good news is that the Holy Spirit can detect each one of them. Pray to receive that vital provision of the Spirit! The church's greatest concern is not from without. It is from within. And that threat takes two very dangerous forms. The first is "soulishness"; that is, pride and pageantry taking the place of true spirituality. This is a subtle imitation of the Spirit which many unwary souls cannot detect. The next threat is much more shameless and brazen.

On January 30, 1998, the Episcopal Diocese of Newark, New Jersey, in an overwhelming vote of 115–35, by its clergy and 234–128 by its laity, gave official church blessing to homosexuality and non-married relations. Nearly five hundred years ago Martin Luther put this action in perspective when he wrote:

> If I profess with the loudest voice and the clearest exposition every portion of the truth of God except precisely that little point which the world and the devil are at that moment attacking, I am not confessing Christ, however boldly I may be professing Christ. Where the battle rages, there the loyalty of the soldiers is proved. And to be steady on all the battle fronts besides is mere flight and disgrace, if the soldier flinches at that one point.

Liberalism has gutted many mainline denominational churches and left them in hellish unbelief. In many evangelical, fundamental churches, denominational interpretation has produced the same results. Though it is not usually recognized, the effects of liberalism and fundamentalism are similar. The first denies the inspiration of all Scripture; the second denies only selected parts. Both

are deadly. One produces rebellion; the other creates religious legalism. Churches from each group will continue
to die, as will some full-gospel congregations. Every week
some fifty to sixty churches from various denominations
in the United States permanently close their doors.[1]
While New Testament-style revival is sweeping across
other nations and thousands are being converted, here at
home most of the church is in a dangerously languid state.
We are in a period of historic transition. Cultural
Christianity is passing out of the scene. Authentic
Christianity is returning and will ultimately assume its
rightful place.

Chapter Ten

Spiritual Warfare: You Have Authority Over Demons

A rguments flare over the issue of whether or not Christians can be indwelt by demons. First of all, the question is not one of possession or ownership. Christians *cannot* be owned by demons. The Greek word *daimonidzomai*, translated as "demonized" in the New Testament, regards harassment and vexation by demons; it has no implication of ownership. Therefore, Christians cannot be possessed by demons. But Christians *can* be internally harassed by demons, and frequently are. Depression, divorce, disease, violence, poverty, persistent failure–these are only a few of their works.

Some people deny the reality of believers suffering demonic indwelling because it conflicts with other doctrines. Conflicting or not, Paul explained that our corruptible has not yet "put on incorruption," and our mortal has not yet "put on immortality" (1 Cor. 15:54). Until that happens, unclean spirits can go wherever sin and disease go. The sooner we face up to that reality, the sooner we can get on with kingdom work. Our mission is to rescue those taken captive by powers of darkness. (See 2 Timothy 2:25–26.)

Proof texts of Christians' vulnerability to demons are these:

1. Jesus rebuked the disciples and said, "You do not know what manner of *spirit* you are of" (Luke 9:55, emphasis added).

2. "For if he who comes preaches another Jesus whom we have not preached, or if you receive a different *spirit* which you have not received..." (2 Cor. 11:4, emphasis added).

3. "[Jesus] turned and said to Peter, 'Get behind Me, *Satan*! You are an offense to Me...'" (Matt. 16:23, emphasis added).

4. "A woman who had a *spirit* of infirmity eighteen years and was bent over... was made straight" (Luke 13:11–13, emphasis added).

On several occasions I ministered deliverance to people who were demonized, totally out of their minds, and had to be physically restrained by paramedics, policemen, firemen and medical doctors. In each instance the victims were set free. On one such occasion, after a hellish hour-long battle in which the demons spoke and displayed super-human strength (See Mark 5:3–5.), the policemen returned to their station and filed the report: "We witnessed a successful exorcism." The experience made believers of them.

Unfortunately, the *National Enquirer* and several other tabloids published the account nationwide. The real tragedy, however, is that secular papers will capitalize on such Christian stories while church publications maintain a deathly silence. Many denominations want no part of a miracle-working Jesus; it is less disturbing to keep their problem than change their doctrine. Years after this young man's deliverance, a stranger came to my office, introduced himself, and said, "You don't recognize me, but I am the fireman who helped hold that boy on the bed that night. That made a believer out of me! I'm now a Bible-quoting Christian."

The Extension of Jesus' Authority to the Body of Christ

1. Jesus "called His twelve disciples together and gave them power and authority over all demons, and to cure diseases" (Luke 9:1).
2. "I give you the authority to trample on serpents and scorpions, and over all the power of the enemy, and nothing shall by any means hurt you" (Luke 10:19).
3. "These signs will follow those who believe: In My name they will cast out demons" (Mark 16:17).
4. "The weapons of our warfare are not carnal but mighty in God for pulling down strongholds" (2 Cor. 10:3–4).
5. "Put on the whole armor of God, that you may be able to stand against the wiles of the devil" (Eph. 6:11).
6. "Submit to God. Resist the devil and he will flee from you" (James 4:7).
7. "The God of peace will crush Satan under your feet shortly" (Rom. 16: 20).
8. That you may know "what is the exceeding greatness of His power toward us who believe" (Eph. 1:19).
9. Saints overcome Satan by "the blood of the Lamb and by the word of their testimony, and they [do] not love their lives to the death" (Rev. 12:10–11).

The "destruction of high places" in the Old Testament

(2 Kin. 18:4) and its New Testament counterpart, "pulling down strongholds" (2 Cor. 10:4), is not complete until the altar of God has been rebuilt in its place. (See 1 Kings 18:30.) This means that a person absolutely must refill an abandoned pagan life with the power of Jesus Christ.

Deliverance without self-defense is both ineffective and dangerous. We must be "more than conquerors"; merely capturing and subduing the enemy is not enough. The powers of darkness must be replaced with the powers of holiness, light and truth. Jesus warned that an unclean spirit *will* return and seek re-entry "to his house" (Matt. 12:43–45). The only safety measure is for the person to be:

1. filled with the Holy Spirit,
2. exercise scriptural authority,
3. maintain refuge in the body of Christ.

Thirty percent of Jesus' recorded ministry was spent in direct conflict with unclean spirits. Compare that fact with the unwillingness of today's church to admit the reality of the problem. We must not regard ourselves as intellectually inferior or feel apologetic because we believe the whole testimony of Scripture. Jesus dealt with unclean spirits, and so must we.

Interestingly, the secular world is moving ahead of many churches in this regard. Dr. M. Scott Peck, Harvard-educated psychiatrist and author of a number of books, tells of his conversion to belief in demons. He wrote: "An expression appeared on the patient's face that could be described only as satanic... The fact of the matter is that I didn't feel that I could address the subject of evil with integrity without dealing with the question, 'Is there such a thing as an evil spirit?'... When I started researching, I didn't really think that there was and then I gradually discovered that there was."[1]

Successful deliverance depends upon the person's submission to God, forgiveness of others and resistance of the devil. (See James 4:7.) He must repent of all occult practices of the past, renounce every cult that denies the blood of Jesus Christ and recant all philosophies which do not acknowledge His deity. Any book or article related to demonism must be destroyed. (See Deuteronomy 7:26; Acts 19:19.)

Binding and Loosing in the Spirit-Realm

Demons will sometimes integrate with a person's personality to the degree that the individual can no longer separate his self-identity from that of the demon. When this occurs, the person may legitimately feel that he "cannot change." The attitude becomes, "This is just the way I am... What you see is the real me... Don't expect me to do what is not in my power," and so on. This is frequently true with alcoholics who accepted the idea that they themselves are the root problem. Some even find comfort in taking the blame rather than putting it on a spirit.

Spirits that control the mind dominate to the degree that the person fears the change that deliverance would bring; the victim cannot comprehend his identity as continuing to exist apart from the spirit. In many instances, the two have cooperated together for such a long period that in the victim's mind they have become indistinguishably one. In this case, it is much harder to gain the cooperation of the person and for him to recognize his need for deliverance. Quietly, but authoritatively, bind the spirits in the name of Jesus. My usual procedure is to "bind, rebuke, banish." Encourage the person to drop all resistance, yield fully to God and submit to the ministry. He is absolutely safe in trusting the Holy Spirit. When that has been done,

I have never known a deliverance ministry to fail.

1. "Whatever you bind on earth will be bound in heaven, and whatever you loose on earth will be loosed in heaven" (Matt. 16:19).
2. "He first binds the strongman... then plunder his house" (Matt. 12:29).
3. "Ought not this woman... whom Satan has bound... these eighteen years, be loosed from this bond on the Sabbath?" (Luke 13:16).
4. "Let the saints... bind their kings with chains, and their nobles with fetters of iron; To execute on them the written judgment—This honor have all His saints" (Ps. 149:5, 8–9).

The Early Church Fathers' Experience With Unclean Spirits

Tertullian (A.D. 160–225) in his apology to the rulers of the Roman Empire said:

Let a person be brought before your tribunals who is plainly under demoniacal possession. The wicked spirit, bidden to speak by a follower of Christ, will as readily make the truthful confession that he is a demon, as elsewhere he has falsely asserted that he is a god. Or, if you will, let there be produced one of the god-possessed, as they are supposed—if they do not confess, in their fear of lying to a Christian, that they are demons, then and there shed the blood of that most impudent follower of Christ. All the authority and power we have over them is from our naming the Name of Christ, and recalling to their memory the woes with which God threatens them at the hand of Christ their Judge, and which they expect one day to overtake them. Fearing Christ in God and God in Christ, they become subject to the servants of God and Christ. So at one touch and breathing, overwhelmed by the thought and realization of those judgment fires, they leave at our command the bodies they have entered, unwilling, and distressed, and before your very eyes, put to an open shame...[2]

Justin Martyr (A.D. 100–165), in his second apology addressed to the Roman Senate, says:

Numberless demoniacs throughout the whole world and in your city, many of our Christian men—exorcising them in the name of Jesus Christ who was crucified under Pontius Pilate—have healed and do heal, rendering helpless, and driving the possessing demon out of the men, though they could not be cured by all other exorcists, and those who use incantations and drugs.[3]

Cyprian (A.D. 200–258) declared,

Nevertheless, these evil spirits adjured by the living God immediately obey us, submit to us, acknowledge our power, and are forced to come out of the bodies they possess.

These apostolic fathers lived into the third century after Christ and ministered long after the death of the original twelve; none believed the Holy Spirit's power had diminished. Quite the opposite, they continued in the same pattern which Jesus gave. In a very different pattern, the modern church has yet to comprehend the tragic loss it has forced upon those who trusted themselves to its care. No one is more guilty than I was.

When I was pastor in Atlanta in the early 1960s, an attractive young woman joined our congregation and became active in the single adult fellowship. Her father was a well-known minister in our denomination, and her presence was appreciated by everyone. She was quiet, sweet, and soon married a young man with a professional career. Her home was comfortable, and they were blessed with four beautiful children. About a year after I left the church, I was shocked to read in the newspaper that she had killed her husband, all of her children, and committed suicide. While the family was asleep, she loaded her gun, then methodically shot her husband and each child. Afterward, she took her own life. It was a bizarre murder that numbed the city of Atlanta and, to my knowledge, still holds the record for being the worst murder-suicide in Atlanta's history.

I still grieve for that young woman and the terror that devastated her life. At the time I was her pastor, I knew nothing about the power of the Holy Spirit or spiritual warfare. Like most denominations, mine did not teach about the gifts of the Spirit or the imparting of His authority. Even so, I blame no one but myself. I should have discovered those truths. Too late I realized that the demon rampaging in her could have been cast out. Had I, her father, other pastors or believers been operating in New Testament authority, she and her family could be alive today. The gift of discerning of spirits could have identified the presence of the demons before the tragedy occurred.

Occasionally, I hear some television or radio evangelist scorning the miraculous works of God. I weep for these men. More than that, I weep for their congregations and the needless depravation they will experience. Operating in the power of the Holy Spirit is not a luxury the church can accept or reject. People's lives are at stake. The gifts of the Spirit are essential. It was my ignorance and that of others that allowed the devil to destroy that young woman and her family. Having to admit my failure still grieves my heart. The worse grief, however, is for those who deliberately reject God's Word and turn from the Holy Spirit's empowering. I have been on both sides of this religious fence and have seen the consequence each side has to offer. For that reason, I want no more of the utter waste which comes from a powerless gospel. My pathway to New Testament truth came from a background of great loss. This young woman's catastrophe is not the only incident from which I draw my feelings.

The positive side is that I have seen wonderful success in ministering through the power of the Spirit to other crisis situations. A pastor who was battling severe depression came to us for ministry. Though we did not know it, he also brought his gun. Another brother and I ministered deliverance to him and cast out the spirit of depression. Afterward, he told us about the gun and said, "I had made up my mind that if this ministry failed, I was not going home alive." Thankfully, he is doing well today and has a successful ministry.

On another occasion, I received an early morning telephone call from a woman whose only child had just committed suicide. As we talked, the mother held a gun in her lap and was desperately trying not to take her own life. When I brought the authority of Jesus against the spirit of suicide, it left, and the woman was filled with the joy of the Lord. She is a vibrant, happy Christian today.

One man who killed his wife received deliverance in my office while on his way to prison. His wife could be alive today, and he a free man, had he accepted help sooner. His pattern of ignoring the need and postponing deliverance is typical of many. Even ministers who know the truth sometimes reject the power gifts of the Holy Spirit until it becomes *their* wife, son, daughter, friend, or loved one who has been destroyed. I plead with you: Do not make that mistake.

I could tell of many more who have found freedom in Christ. Suicidals, homosexuals, drug addicts, child beaters, pornography victims, amnesiacs, people with multiple personalities, compulsive liars and a long list of others have been set free.

While I have no hesitation to minister deliverance publicly, many times I prefer it be done privately. Only those persons authorized by the pastor and elders should participate in the ministry. Others should pray but not become directly involved.

Remember that the person receiving ministry is frightened and may feel publicly exposed. He or she needs to be comforted and protected. Do not lapse into personal talk or mannerism which detracts from the spiritual sense of urgency or privacy. Even when such people appear to be unconscious or unable to communicate, they can usually hear. Speak to them reassuringly, encourage them, ask for their cooperation. Some ministries may require more time than is presently available. When that occurs, bind the spirits in the authority of Jesus' name (See Matthew 12:29.), discontinue the ministry temporarily, and resume later.

Smelling a Wolf in the Dark

I meet Christians who are virtually powerless in the area of discernment. They excel in their love for God, but in detecting Satan's devices, they remain spiritually naive. Theoretically, what these Christians observe in daylight hours, they recognize well. When darkness falls, they are helpless as anyone else, easily victimized by "the trickery of men" (Eph. 4:14). When the thief comes "to steal, and to kill, and to destroy" (John 10:10), they are quickly exploited. The high divorce rate among Christians is primary proof of what I say. Deception rips good couples apart. Families, individuals, even churches frequently have long histories of wrong decision-making. This cannot be the will of God. He is not honored when the world makes fools of His children.

Scripture has provided adequate protection against this hazard through the Holy Spirit's gift of discerning of spirits. (See 1 Corinthians 12:10.) But this gift does not operate automatically; it has to be nourished and lovingly developed. A casual attitude toward it will produce superficial results; an earnest seeking of it will bring remarkable discretion and judgment. The choice is ours. In the New Testament day, the word *discern* was a Greek medical term which meant "to cut and look below the surface." With this spiritual gift in operation, one does not merely rely on things as they *appear* but may know them as they really *are*. Thankfully, it is possible for believers to receive revelations from the Holy Spirit.

To illustrate scripturally the operation of discerning of spirits, we need to compare quotations of Isaiah 11:1–3, from both the old and New King James Bibles. You will observe that these two versions use very different language in translating the same word. Here is a partial quote from the original King James:

> And there shall come forth a rod out of the stem of Jesse, and a Branch shall grow out of his roots: And the Spirit of the Lord shall rest upon him… and shall make him of *quick understanding* in the fear of the Lord: and he shall not judge after the sight of his eyes, neither reprove after the hearing of his ears (Isa. 11:1–3, emphasis added).

Where the original King James says, "Shall make him of *quick understanding* in the fear of the Lord," the New King James says, "His *delight* is in the fear of the Lord." "Quick understanding" and "delight" seem contradictory translations. The Hebrew word *ruach* is the source for

169

each, and both are valid renderings. Their combined messages bring a valuable revelation about discerning of spirits. *Ruach* is translated as "spirit, wind, breath." (See Genesis 1:1.) When translated as "delight" in the New King James, *ruach* refers to the inhaled breath; specifically, as "the delight of inhaling the fragrance of roses." The original King James, instead of referring to the *pleasure* of smelling, refers to the *result*. For example:

In ancient Israel, sheepherding was a vital part of life. During the day, it was easy for the shepherd or sheep dog to see a wolf and protect the flock. Nighttime was a different story; when darkness fell, the shepherd was powerless. Not so with the dog. Even in the dark, when he could not "judge after the sight of his eyes or reprove after the hearing of his ears," the dog could *smell* a wolf.

It was this usage of *ruach* which Isaiah said would typify the future Messiah. When Messiah came, He would not depend on sight or hearing for making judgment; instead, another sense, one which could penetrate the dark, would be His basis of judgment. When the Scripture says, "The Spirit of the LORD shall... make him of quick understanding," that is, "quick to smell," it literally means the Messiah will be able to "smell a wolf in the dark." Those who operate in this charisma gift do not find themselves defenseless simply because night has fallen.

The story is told of a famous English minister who preached in the London Armory. A lady once interrupted him and said they needed to leave the building. The speaker obeyed, everyone filed out, and they had gotten a short distance from the armory when it exploded. Gunpowder stored in the building detonated and demolished the structure. Had they remained inside they would have been killed. Did the woman experience a discerning of spirits or a word of knowledge? I don't know. I only know I want whatever she had. Nor will I argue with God and say that such miraculous gifts "passed away." You shouldn't either, unless you want to blow up.

I am not saying we will function perfectly in any of the gifts; I certainly do not. At best, we are imperfect vessels. What I am saying is that we can function much better than we are presently doing. Nor do we seek gifts of our own choosing. We seek the Giver, then we are free to tell Him the areas in which we feel our greatest need. Let me ask you a personal question: Have there been times in your life when you made imprudent, costly mistakes, because you depended on your eyes and ears and not your heart? The answer, of course, is yes. We all are guilty. Were there other times when you had a deep "sense of warning" which you ignored? Again, all of us must admit that we have. Had you known that God had a provision to protect you from many of those blunders, would you have accepted it?

Discerning of spirits is only part of the Holy Spirit's package. (See Acts 1:4-8; 1 Corinthians 12:14.) There are other endowments which come with it. All are wonderful, good, precious, blessings from heaven. Even so, some well-intended but wrongly motivated Christians scorn them. Not every church or denomination believes in the "packaging of the gifts"—the baptism in the Holy Spirit.

In fighting spiritual gifts, we Christians merely wound ourselves. God says these gifts are real. More importantly, He wants us to have them. They are part of Jesus' provision for the church. In our denial, we leave ourselves wide open for more deception by the wolf. (See Acts 20:29.) If you want spiritual gifts, they are yours for the asking—provided you will love, treasure, nourish and encourage them. That requires submission to the total New Testament message. It requires time in prayer, fasting, communion with the Holy Spirit. Pride, ego, self-seeking, carnal ambition must go.

Frequently Asked Questions About Demonic Manifestations

Q. What should be done for children who witness demonic manifestations?

A. First of all, children are continually exposed to demonic activity on television, at school and in other public places without recognizing it as such or being instructed about it. The church is the only place where they can see the power of God in action and being victorious over powers of darkness. For that reason, there are positive effects in children's witnessing the deliverance of a tormented person. They can see both the ugliness of the devil's work and the beauty of Jesus. In every case, children need to be personally reminded that the power of Jesus is greater than the power of the enemy and that they do not need to be afraid. Even so, children need to be protected from fear entering them by having adult believers pray over them and rebuking any spirit that tries to take advantage of their vulnerability.

Q. When demons leave a person is it possible for them to enter any person of their choice who is close by?

A. Absolutely not. In this regard, Jesus said, "Nothing shall by any means hurt you." Demons cannot claim any victim they select; they must have legal entry through sinful acts, willful submission to them, ancestral curses, fear and so on.

Q. What should I do to protect myself and my family?

A. Those ministering should always call for the protection of "the blood of Jesus," submit themselves to God, resist the enemy and know that he will flee from them. (See James 4:7.)

Q. What is my source of authority over the devil?

A. The name of Jesus, the Word of God, the Holy Spirit's indwelling and the blood of the Lamb. Each time Satan tempted Jesus in the wilderness, Jesus answered by saying, "It is written!... It is written!... It is written!" We too must know the Word of God and use it!

Q. What is a major pitfall to avoid?

A. Jesus never said believers "will try to cast out demons." He said, "They will." We do not try. Through His empowering, we do it. "Greater is He who is in us than he who is in the world." Do not allow others to rob your faith. Be forewarned. Emotion is not faith. The devil is not intimidated by noise. He responds only to the authority of Jesus.

Chapter Eleven

Finale: Release of Power From Your Inner Person

The opening of the disciples' understanding to Scripture-revelation did not occur when Jesus breathed into them saying, "Receive the Holy Spirit" (John 20:22). Nor did it occur on the Day of Pentecost when they were "endued with power from on high." (See Acts 2.) Mighty as were these events, they did *not* unveil Scripture-truth to the disciples. This is an important observation. It is possible to be born again and baptized in the Spirit without having one's understanding opened to *revelation-knowledge*. This is verified in our day by many who have experienced the new birth and Spirit's baptism without moving into the deeper revelation of His truth. That should concern us. Observe how Jesus opened the disciples' understanding on the road to Emmaus: "Then He said to them, 'These are the words which I spoke to you while I was still with you, that all things must be fulfilled which were written in the Law of Moses and the Prophets and the Psalms concerning Me.' And He opened their understanding, that they might comprehend the Scriptures" (Luke 24:44–45). "And they said to one another, 'Did not our heart burn within us while He talked with us on the road, and while He *opened* the Scriptures to us?'" (24:32).

In various forms, the verb *open* appears 106 times in the New Testament. The specific word translated here, *dianoigo*, is used only seven times. It means "to open thoroughly," as the opening of the womb in giving birth. (See Luke 2:23.) Some things can be opened and closed repeatedly without permanent change. This is not true with *dianoigo*. Once opened, as in the case of the womb, it can never be closed and returned to its original state. The disciples' experience of having "their understanding opened to comprehend the Scriptures" was an opening of that magnitude. For them and for us, such an opening is absolutely necessary before we can become capable preachers of the New Testament. Paul said, "God has made us able ministers of the New Testament, not of the letter, but of the Spirit. For the letter kills but the Spirit gives life" (2 Cor. 6:6). The preponderance of "letter" preaching with the absence of the Spirit's revelation is a deadly blight on modern Christianity. It is the source of much legalism and doctrinal feuding.

In ancient Israel, God had His own method for opening the ear; a blessing which was reserved only for those who voluntarily became permanent bond-slaves. (See Deuteronomy 15:12–18; Exodus 21:1–6.) One who accepted a life of immutable servitude was brought to the doorpost and with hammer and spike, nailed to the frame of the house. Once this decision was made, it was irrevocable. The rite expressed these spiritual facts:

1. Heart-commitment to the Master.
2. Willingness to endure pain.
3. Shedding of one's own blood.

4. Permanent scarring of the body.
5. Piercing of the ear.

The most vital message in this ceremony was the fact that the servant's blood was shed on the *doorpost*; that spot reserved for the blood of the Great Servant—the Passover Lamb. No other blood ever dared go there. Kings, High Priests, Governors, were denied this privilege. The message to the New Testament believer is this: If you genuinely want God's opening in your ear, your personal *dianoigo*, and your entrance into revelation knowledge, there is only one way to receive it. You surrender your right to the self-life of ego, pride, dignity, control; in its place receive a scar. You permanently become a bond-slave. But the reward is matchless; you then have God's opening in your spiritual ear. Like the disciples on the Emmaus Road, your heart will "burn within you" while He "opens the Scripture" to your understanding. You will then have "an ear to hear what the Spirit is saying to the churches" (Rev. 2:7).

God Wants You to Receive Spiritual Wisdom and Knowledge

1. "And the LORD said to Moses: 'Take Joshua the son of Nun with you, a man in whom is the Spirit, and lay your hand on him'" (Num. 27:18).
2. "Now Joshua the son of Nun was full of the spirit of wisdom, for Moses had laid his hands on him" (Deut. 34:9).
3. "That the God of our Lord Jesus Christ, the Father of glory, may give to you the spirit of wisdom and revelation in the knowledge of Him, the eyes of your understanding being enlightened; that you may know what is the hope of His calling, what are the riches of the glory of His inheritance in the saints, and what is the exceeding greatness of His power toward us who believe,

according to the working of His mighty power" (Eph. 1:17).

4. "He who has an ear, let him hear what the Spirit says to the churches" (Rev. 3:6). This exhortation was spoken seven times in the first three chapters of Revelation.

5. "He answered and said to them, 'Because it has been given to you to know the mysteries of the kingdom of heaven...'" (Matt. 13:11).

The struggle to hear what "the Spirit is saying to the church" is not an easy one. All of us are much more insulated to His voice than we realize. After my encounter with the Holy Spirit in 1977, phenomenal as it was, I discovered I was much like Lazarus, alive but still tightly wrapped in grave clothes. (See John 11:44.) In a progressive way, God began dealing with my wrong attitudes. One great event occurred when my wife, daughter and I visited the Grand Tetons and Yellowstone National Park. This is undoubtedly one of the most scenic spots in America, and we stayed at the Jackson Hole Lodge with its enormous picture window facing the mountains. I was awed by the scenery.

One evening I left the hotel and climbed a hill on the north side to spend time in prayer. Though the plain was no longer visible, I could still see the silhouette of mountains in the distance. It was a beautiful moment of fellowship with nature and God. Without any forewarning, the Lord suddenly broke into my quiet and said, "I want you to give up your *right* to be angry." There was no explanation, just that simple instruction, "Give up your *right* to be angry." I was shocked. It was not merely an impression; it was a verbal message. I also knew what He meant. I was angry—and though I had concealed it, I had carried that anger a very long time. But, He had not asked me to "give up my anger." Instead, He carefully said to give up my *right* to be angry. That told me several things: God not only knew I had justifiable grounds to be angry, but more importantly, He knew if I gave up anger without giving up my "right" to it, that it would quickly return.

My major problem was that I did not *want* to give up my right.

Anger gave me a sense of power and control which I felt I needed.

For several minutes I struggled with the instruction. Finally, I realized that my anger was in direct competition with God's will. If I wanted Him to take command of the circumstances that troubled me, I would have to give up my right to it. I wish I could tell you that my decision was quick and easy. But it was not. Finally, I said, "Alright, Lord, I'll do it. I give up my right to be angry. I turn loose and trust You to take over." It was that simple, almost emotionless.

When I went back to the hotel, I said nothing to my wife and daughter. Though I did not realize it, that was one of the most historic moments of my life. Immediately, I saw dramatic changes take place in every area surrounding me. Church problems were transformed; personal difficulties disappeared. I became less self-defensive, more laid-back, less responsive to attack. My ministry soared to a new plane as the gifts and power of the Holy Spirit found release. Another part of me had died. In my case, anger had been a key. For you, it may be something else. For all of us, the results of surrendering our egos to God is the same.

God does not want us to be broken; He does want the *benefits of brokenness* in us. If we voluntarily yield to the remolding process of the Holy Spirit, we can escape the painful consequence of disobedience. For years afterward, I kept a picture of the Grand Tetons on my office wall. It was there as a constant reminder of the change God brought into my life. It was also there for others who came for ministry. As I told them the story, applying it to the ego-issue in their life, many experienced the same freedom that had come to me. They saw that pride, self-will, anger and all ego-related sin are in direct opposition to the work of God. These controllers are abortive, destructive, hell-induced traits which battle against the Holy Spirit's mission in us.

Soon after the Grand Tetons experience, I was on Lookout Mountain in Georgia one Autumn morning when the trees were in their full glory; they had a glow that seemed to come from deep within. As I held several leaves, the Holy Spirit spoke to me. The message was not about leaves, but about those who wish to be instruments of His power.

A few days before, I had learned that Autumn colors do not come into the leaves because they are dying. Instead, the reds, golds and green all came into the leaves in the spring and have been present all summer long. When cooler nights stop the manufacture of chlorophyll in the fall, the green fades, and the more beautiful colors are free to appear. The revelation the Holy Spirit gave me that day is that we too, have a visible, or "natural body," and an invisible, or "spiritual body" (1 Cor. 15:44). Our outer-person, which was typified by the green, is easily seen; the other is the "hidden man of the heart," and frequently remains concealed. Both natures exist simultaneously in us, but, as in the case of the trees, our "outer person" over-powers the "inner man of the spirit" and prevents his being seen. What I saw in a flash is that *the anointing is only released through the inner person.* That cannot happen until, like the Autumn colors, he has been set free.

In that moment, I realized that much activity, ministry, worship, is attempted through the medium of the outer man. The inner-person of the spirit, through which Jesus works, remains obscured. We are unable to do the "works of the Spirit" because we try to accomplish them in the chlorophyll of our soulish green. It will not work. The Holy Spirit showed me, identically as in the Autumn leaves, the inner-man of the spirit is released only in proportion to the death of the outer man. When the natural man is still strong, making decisions, giving orders, the results may appear authentic, but in reality, they are an imitation of the Holy Spirit's true work. When ego has been slain and its nature subdued, the believer may then become the instrument through whom the power of the Spirit is liberated. Not until. The Holy Spirit will not compete with our soulishness. What appears as "power" in people who are still motivated by pride is only a hint of what the Spirit would do if their vessels were truly emptied of self.

There are various ways which the New Testament identifies this crucifying of the self-life and the releasing of God's power in us. Without question, it means that we voluntarily become "crucified with Christ" (Gal. 2:20). This is not a death to dread; rather, it is an offer of grace toward which we should run. Instead of a dying experience, it is a birthing experience. In the analogy of Autumn leaves, it simply means that our green must go. The spiritual person in us must come forth. When God showed me this truth, I hurriedly wrote these lines.

> Of all the things that die,
> Ego dies the hardest;
> There is no heart-arrest,
> No sudden stopping of the breath,
> Just a slow and painful grieving,
> As ego feels its powers leaving;
> Struggling against the dreaded Cross,
> Wrongly thinking death is loss;
> But, if, and when, it dies in grief,
> How welcome is that sweet relief!

It is God's will that you be baptized, filled and empowered with every potential of the Holy Spirit. In experiencing that, you will become one of those of whom the Scripture says, "The Lord working with them and confirming the word through the accompanying signs" (Mark 16:20). God wants you as an effective witness to a world desperately needing the "demonstration of the Spirit and power" (1 Cor. 2:4). This is your most urgent, personal need. For that to happen, you must be as open to the Holy Spirit as a flower is to a bee. Let Him have access to your deepest part. He *will* endue you with His greatness.

Come with Jesus up the mountain. Experience your own "Mount of Transfiguration" (Matt. 17:1–8). From that encounter, return to public life, changed and glowing in the power of the Holy Spirit. As He slips Covenant bracelets on your wrists, you will "taste the heavenly gift," become "partakers of the Holy Spirit" and step into the "powers of the age to come" (Heb. 6:4–5). In surrendering your will to His, He will plunge you into a depth of the Holy Spirit you have never known before. You too, will stand with your feet on earth, your face in heaven, as He reveals the mysteries of the kingdom. His power will fill you and flow through you in ways you never thought possible. Grace in its fullest dimension becomes your living reality.

You have everything to gain and nothing to lose. You may ask, cry or beg many times, but you need *surrender only once.* Let go, and let God. Trust Him totally. Rest in the truth of His Word. Prayerfully, do that by letting the words of the following old hymn express your new submission to Christ. You may have sung it a thousand times—or it may be new—but its truth is eternal. And the blessing of surrendering to Jesus as Baptizer (See John 1:33.), can be yours. Heaven is waiting to hear you say,

All to Jesus I surrender,
Lord I give myself to Thee;
Fill me with Thy love and power,
Let Thy Blessing fall on me.
I surrender all, I surrender all,
All to Thee, my blessed Savior,
I surrender all!

—Judson W. VanDeVenter

Welcome to the "Edge of Glory."

Appendix A: The Ministry of the Holy Spirit

1. "I indeed baptize you with water unto repentance, but He who is coming after me is mightier than I, whose sandals I am not worthy to carry. He will baptize you with the Holy Spirit and fire" (Matt. 3:11).

2. "Anyone who speaks a word against the Son of Man, it will be forgiven him; but whoever speaks against the Holy Spirit, it will not be forgiven him, either in this age or in the age to come" (Matt. 12:32).

3. "I indeed baptized you with water, but He will baptize you with the Holy Spirit" (Mark 1:8).

4. "But when they arrest you and deliver you up, do not worry beforehand, or premeditate what you will speak. But whatever is given you in that hour, speak that; for it is not you who speak, but the Holy Spirit" (Mark 13:11).

5. "Now his father Zacharias was filled with the Holy Spirit, and prophesied" (Luke 1:67).

6. "And the Holy Spirit descended in bodily form like a dove upon Him, and a voice came from heaven which said, "You are My beloved Son; in You I am well pleased" (Luke 3:22).

7. "If you then, being evil, know how to give good gifts to your children, how much more will your heavenly Father give the Holy Spirit to those who ask Him!" Luke 11:13.

8. "For the Holy Spirit will teach you in that very hour what you ought to say" (Luke 12:12).

9. "But this He spoke concerning the Spirit, whom those believing in Him would receive; for the Holy Spirit was not yet given, because Jesus was not yet glorified" (John 7:39).

10. "But the Helper, the Holy Spirit, whom the Father will send in My name, He will teach you all things, and bring to your remembrance all things that I said to you" (John 14:26).

11. "And when He had said this, He breathed on them, and said to them, 'Receive the Holy Spirit'" (John 20:22).

12. "Until the day in which He was taken up, after He through the Holy Spirit had given commandments to the apostles whom He had chosen" (Acts 1:2).

13. "For John truly baptized with water, but you shall be baptized with the Holy Spirit not many days from now" (Acts 1:5).

14. "But you shall receive power when the Holy Spirit has come upon you; and you shall be witnesses to Me in Jerusalem, and in all Judea and Samaria, and to the end of the earth" (Acts 1:8).

15. "And they were all filled with the Holy Spirit and began to speak with other tongues, as the Spirit gave them utterance" (Acts 2:4).

16. "Therefore being exalted to the right hand of God, and having received from the Father the promise of the Holy Spirit, He poured out this which you now see and hear" (Acts 2:33).

17. "Then Peter said to them, 'Repent, and let every one of you be baptized in the name of Jesus Christ for the remission of sins; and you shall receive the gift of the Holy Spirit'" (Acts 2:38).

18. "And when they had prayed, the place where they were assembled together was shaken; and they were all filled with the Holy Spirit, and they spoke the word of God with boldness" (Acts 4:31).

19. "But Peter said, 'Ananias, why has Satan filled your heart to lie to the Holy Spirit and keep back part of the price of the land for yourself?'" (Acts 5:3).

20. "And we are His witnesses to these things, and so also is the Holy Spirit whom God has given to those who obey Him" (Acts 5:32).

21. "You stiff-necked and uncircumcised in heart and ears! You always resist the Holy Spirit; as your fathers did, so do you" (Acts 7:51).

22. "Who, when they had come down, prayed for them that they might receive the Holy Spirit" (Acts 8:15).

23. "Then they laid hands on them, and they received the Holy Spirit" (Acts 8:17).

24. "And when Simon saw that through the laying on of the apostles' hands the Holy Spirit was given, he offered them money" (Acts 8:18).

25. "Give me this power also, that anyone on whom I lay hands may receive the Holy Spirit" (Acts 8:19).

26. "And Ananias went his way and entered the house; and laying his hands on him he said, 'Brother Saul, the Lord Jesus, who appeared to you on the road as you came, has sent me that you may receive your sight and be filled with the Holy Spirit'" (Acts 9:17).

27. "God anointed Jesus of Nazareth with the Holy Spirit and with power, who went about doing good and healing all who were oppressed by the devil, for God was with Him" (Acts 10:38).

28. "While Peter was still speaking these words, the Holy Spirit fell upon all those who heard the word. And those of the circumcision who believed were astonished, as many as came with Peter, because the gift of the Holy Spirit had been poured out on the Gentiles also" (Acts 10:44–45).

29. "Can anyone forbid water, that these should not be baptized who have received the Holy Spirit just as we have?" (Acts 10:47).

30. "As they ministered to the Lord and fasted, the Holy Spirit said, "Now separate to Me Barnabas and Saul for the work to which I have called them" (Acts 13:2).

31. "So, being sent out by the Holy Spirit, they went down to Seleucia, and from there they sailed to Cyprus" (Acts 13:4).

32. "He said to them, 'Did you receive the Holy Spirit when you believed?' So they said to him, 'We have not so much as heard whether there is a Holy Spirit'" (Acts 19:2).

33. "And when Paul had laid hands on them, the Holy Spirit came upon them, and they spoke with tongues and prophesied" (Acts 19:6).

34. "Except that the Holy Spirit testifies in every city, saying that chains and tribulations await me" (Acts 20:23).

35. "For the kingdom of God is not eating and drinking, but righteousness and peace and joy in the Holy Spirit" (Rom. 14:17).

36. "Therefore I make known to you that no one speaking by the Spirit of God calls Jesus accursed, and no one can say that Jesus is Lord except by the Holy Spirit" (1 Cor. 12:3).

37. "The grace of the Lord Jesus Christ, and the love of God, and the communion of the Holy Spirit be with you all. Amen" (2 Cor. 13:14).

38. "In Him you also trusted, after you heard the word of truth, the gospel of your salvation; in whom also, having believed, you were sealed with the Holy Spirit of promise" (Eph. 1:13).

39. "And do not grieve the Holy Spirit of God, by whom you were sealed for the day of redemption" (Eph. 4:30).

40. "For our gospel did not come to you in word only, but also in power, and in the Holy Spirit and in much assurance, as you know what kind of men we were among you for your sake" (1 Thess. 1:5).

41. "Therefore he who rejects this does not reject man, but God, who has also given us His Holy Spirit" (1 Thess. 4:8).

42. "Not by works of righteousness which we have done, but according to His mercy He saved us, through the washing of regeneration and renewing of the Holy Spirit" (Titus 3:5).

43. "God also bearing witness both with signs and wonders, with various miracles, and gifts of the Holy Spirit, according to His own will?" (Heb. 2:4).

44. "For it is impossible for those who were once enlightened, and have tasted the heavenly gift, and have become partakers of the Holy Spirit, and have tasted the good word of God and the powers of the age to come" (Heb. 6:4).

45. "For prophecy never came by the will of man, but holy men of God spoke as they were moved by the Holy Spirit" (2 Pet. 1:21).

46. "But you, beloved, building yourselves up on your most holy faith, praying in the Holy Spirit" (Jude 1:20).

47. "I was in the Spirit on the Lord's Day" (Rev. 1:10).

48. "He who has an ear, let him hear what the Spirit says to the churches" (Rev. 2:29).

49. "So He carried me away in the Spirit into the wilderness" (Rev. 17:3).

50. "And the Spirit and the bride say, 'Come!' And let him who hears say, 'Come!' And let him who thirsts come. AWhoever desires, let him take the water of life freely" (Rev. 22:17).

Appendix B: The Believer's Authority Over Demons

1. "Then the seventy returned with joy, saying, 'Lord, even the demons are subject to us in Your name.' And He said to them, 'I saw Satan fall like lightning from heaven. Behold, I give you the authority to trample on serpents and scorpions, and over all the power of the enemy, and nothing shall by any means hurt you'" (Luke 10:17−19).

2. "And these signs will follow those who believe: In My name they will cast out demons; they will speak with new tongues; they will take up serpents; and if they drink anything deadly, it will by no means hurt them; they will lay hands on the sick, and they will recover... And they went out and preached everywhere, the Lord working with them and confirming the word through the accompanying signs" (Mark 16:17−18, 20).

3. "Let the saints be joyful in glory; let them sing aloud on their beds. Let the high praises of God be in their mouth, and a two-edged sword in their hand, To execute vengeance on the nations, and punishments on the peoples; To bind their kings with chains, and their nobles with fetters of iron; To execute on them the written judgment— this honor have all His saints" (Ps. 149:5−9).

4. "Therefore submit to God. Resist the devil and he will flee from you. Draw near to God and He will draw near to you" (James 4:7−8).

5. "For though we walk in the flesh, we do not war according to the flesh. For the weapons of our warfare are not carnal but mighty in God for pulling down strongholds, casting down arguments and every high thing that exalts itself against the knowledge of God, bringing every thought into captivity to the obedience of Christ, and being ready to punish all disobedience when your obedience is fulfilled" (2 Cor. 10:3−6).

6. "Beloved, do not believe every spirit, but test the spirits, whether they are of God; because many false prophets have gone out into the world. By this you know the Spirit of God: Every spirit that confesses that Jesus Christ has come in the flesh is of God, and every spirit that does not confess that Jesus Christ has come in the flesh is not of God. And this is the spirit of the Antichrist, which you have heard was coming, and is now already in the world" (1 John 4:1–3).

7. "And when He had called His twelve disciples to Him, He gave them power over unclean spirits, to cast them out, and to heal all kinds of sickness and all kinds of disease" (Matt. 10:1).

8. "And they cast out many demons, and anointed with oil many who were sick, and healed them" (Mark 6:13).

9. "Inasmuch then as the children have partaken of flesh and blood, He Himself likewise shared in the same, that through death He might destroy him who had the power of death, that is, the devil, and release those who through fear of death were all their lifetime subject to bondage" (Heb. 2:14–15).

10. "And the God of peace will crush Satan under your feet shortly" (Rom. 16:20).

11. "You shall tread upon the lion and the cobra, The young lion and the serpent you shall trample underfoot" (Ps. 91:13).

12. "...Joshua called for all the men of Israel, and said to the captains of the men of war who went with him, 'Come near, put your feet on the necks of these kings.' And they drew near and put their feet on their necks" (Josh. 10:24).

13. "...For this purpose the Son of God was manifested, that He might destroy the works of the devil" (1 John 3:8).

14. "You are of God, little children, and have overcome them, because He who is in you is greater than he who is in the world" (1 John 4:4).

15. "[That you] may be able to comprehend with all the saints what is the width and length and depth and height—to know the love of Christ which passes knowledge; that you may be filled with all the fullness of God. Now to Him who is able to do exceedingly abundantly above all that we ask or think, according to the power that works in us, to Him be glory in the church by Christ Jesus to all generations, forever and ever" (Eph. 3:18–21).

16. "[That you may be] strengthened with all might, according to His glorious power, for all patience and longsuffering with joy; giving thanks to the Father who has qualified us to be partakers of the inheritance of the saints in the light. He has delivered us from the power of darkness and conveyed us into the kingdom of the Son of His love, in whom we have redemption through His blood, the forgiveness of sins" (Col. 1:11–14).

17. "For the word of God is living and powerful, and sharper than any two-edged sword, piercing even to the division of soul and spirit, and of joints and marrow, and is a discerner of the thoughts and intents of the heart" (Heb. 4:12).

18. "Paul, greatly annoyed, turned and said to the spirit, 'I command you in the name of Jesus Christ to come out of her.' And he came out that very hour" (Acts 16:18).

19. "But rise and stand on your feet; for I have appeared to you for this purpose, to make you a minister and a witness both of the things which you have seen and of the things which I will yet reveal to you. I will deliver you from the Jewish people, as well as from the Gentiles, to whom I now send you, to open their eyes, in order to turn them from darkness to light, and from the power of Satan to God, that they may receive forgiveness of sins and an

inheritance among those who are sanctified by faith in Me" (Acts 26:16–18).

20. "Most assuredly, I say to you, he who believes in Me, the works that I do he will do also; and greater works than these he will do, because I go to My Father" (John 14:12).

21. "Be sober, be vigilant; because your adversary the devil walks about like a roaring lion, seeking whom he may devour. Resist him, steadfast in the faith" (1 Pet. 5:8–9).

22. "And Jesus rebuked the demon, and it came out of him; and the child was cured from that very hour. Then the disciples came to Jesus privately and said, 'Why could we not cast it out?' So Jesus said to them, 'Because of your unbelief; for assuredly, I say to you, if you have faith as a mustard seed, you will say to this mountain, "Move from here to there," and it will move; and nothing will be impossible for you. However, this kind does not go out except by prayer and fasting'" (Matt. 17:18–21).

23. "Then I heard a loud voice saying in heaven, 'Now salvation, and strength, and the kingdom of our God, and the power of His Christ have come, for the accuser of our brethren, who accused them before our God day and night, has been cast down.' And they overcame him by the blood of the Lamb and by the word of their testimony, and they did not love their lives to the death" (Rev. 12:10–11).

24. "O Daniel, man greatly beloved... 'Do not fear, Daniel, for from the first day that you set your heart to under-stand, and to humble yourself before your God, your words were heard; and I have come because of your words. But the prince of the kingdom of Persia withstood me twenty-one days; and behold, Michael, one of the chief princes, came to help me, for I had been left alone there with the kings of Persia'" (Dan. 10:11–13).

25. "And you He made alive, who were dead in trespasses and sins, in which you once walked according to the course of

this world, according to the prince of the power of the air, the spirit who now works in the sons of disobedience" (Eph. 2:1–2).

26. "...Most assuredly, I say to you, whatever you ask the Father in My name He will give you" (John 16:23).

27. "I am He who lives, and was dead, and behold, I am alive forevermore. Amen. And I have the keys of Hades and of Death" (Rev. 1:18).

28. "For God has not given us a spirit of fear, but of power and of love and of a sound mind" (2 Tim. 1:7).

29. "...But has now been revealed by the appearing of our Savior Jesus Christ, who has abolished death and brought life and immortality to light through the gospel" (2 Tim. 1:10).

30. "Yet Michael the archangel, in contending with the devil, when he disputed about the body of Moses, dared not bring against him a reviling accusation, but said, 'The Lord rebuke you!'" (Jude 1:9).

31. "Then some of the itinerant Jewish exorcists took it upon themselves to call the name of the Lord Jesus over those who had evil spirits, saying, 'We exorcise you by the Jesus whom Paul preaches.' Also there were seven sons of Sceva, a Jewish chief priest, who did so. And the evil spirit answered and said, 'Jesus I know, and Paul I know; but who are you?' Then the man in whom the evil spirit was leaped on them, overpowered them, and prevailed against them, so that they fled out of that house naked and wounded. This became known both to all Jews and Greeks dwelling in Ephesus; and fear fell on them all, and the name of the Lord Jesus was magnified" (Acts 19:13–17).

32. "Stand now with your enchantments and the multitude of your sorceries, in which you have labored from your

youth— perhaps you will be able to profit, perhaps you will prevail. You are wearied in the multitude of your counsels; let now the astrologers, the stargazers, and the monthly prognosticators stand up and save you from what shall come upon you. Behold, they shall be as stubble, the fire shall burn them; They shall not deliver themselves from the power of the flame; ...No one shall save you" (Isa. 47:12–15).

33. "And when He had come out of the boat, immediately there met Him out of the tombs a man with an unclean spirit, who had his dwelling among the tombs; and no one could bind him, not even with chains, because he had often been bound with shackles and chains. And the chains had been pulled apart by him, and the shackles broken in pieces; neither could anyone tame him. And always, night and day, he was in the mountains and in the tombs, crying out and cutting himself with stones. When he saw Jesus from afar, he ran and worshiped Him. And he cried out with a loud voice and said, 'What have I to do with You, Jesus, Son of the Most High God? I implore You by God that You do not torment me.' For He said to him, 'Come out of the man, unclean spirit!'" (Mark 5:2–8).

34. "For unclean spirits, crying with a loud voice, came out of many who were possessed; and many who were paralyzed and lame were healed. And there was great joy in that city" (Acts 8:7–8).

35. "When an unclean spirit goes out of a man, he goes through dry places, seeking rest, and finds none. Then he says, 'I will return to my house from which I came.' And when he comes, he finds it empty, swept, and put in order. Then he goes and takes with him seven other spirits more wicked than himself, and they enter and dwell there; and the last state of that man is worse than the first. So shall it also be with this wicked generation" (Matt. 12:43–45).

36. "There are diversities of gifts, but the same Spirit. There are differences of ministries, but the same Lord. And there are diversities of activities, but it is the same God who works all in all. But the manifestation of the Spirit is given to each one for the profit of all: for to one is given the word of wisdom through the Spirit, to another the word of knowledge through the same Spirit, to another faith by the same Spirit, to another gifts of healings by the same Spirit, to another the working of miracles, to another prophecy, to another discerning of spirits, to another different kinds of tongues, to another the interpretation of tongues. But one and the same Spirit works all these things, distributing to each one individually as He wills" (1 Cor. 12:4–11).

37. "The Spirit of the LORD is upon Me, because He has anointed Me to preach the gospel to the poor; He has sent Me to heal the brokenhearted, to proclaim liberty to the captives and recovery of sight to the blind, to set at liberty those who are oppressed; To proclaim the acceptable year of the LORD" (Luke 4:18–19).

Warring Against Powers and Principalities

38. "Finally, my brethren, be strong in the Lord and in the power of His might. Put on the whole armor of God, that you may be able to stand against the wiles of the devil. For we do not wrestle against flesh and blood, but against principalities, against powers, against the rulers of the darkness of this age, against spiritual hosts of wickedness in the heavenly places. Therefore take up the whole armor of God, that you may be able to withstand in the evil day, and having done all, to stand" (Eph. 6:10–13).

39. "That the God of our Lord Jesus Christ, the Father of glory, may give to you the spirit of wisdom and revelation in the knowledge of Him, the eyes of your understanding being enlightened; that you may know what is the hope of

His calling, what are the riches of the glory of His inheritance in the saints, and what is the exceeding greatness of His power toward us who believe, according to the working of His mighty power which He worked in Christ when He raised Him from the dead and seated Him at His right hand in the heavenly places, far above all principality and power and might and dominion, and every name that is named, not only in this age but also in that which is to come. And He put all things under His feet, and gave Him to be head over all things to the church, which is His body, the fullness of Him who fills all in all" (Eph. 1:17–23).

40. "…To make all see what is the fellowship of the mystery, which from the beginning of the ages has been hidden in God who created all things through Jesus Christ; to the intent that now the manifold wisdom of God might be made known by the church to the principalities and powers in the heavenly places, according to the eternal purpose which He accomplished in Christ Jesus our Lord" (Eph. 3:9–11).

41. "He is the image of the invisible God, the firstborn over all creation. For by Him all things were created that are in heaven and that are on earth, visible and invisible, whether thrones or dominions or principalities or powers. All things were created through Him and for Him. And He is before all things, and in Him all things consist" (Col. 1:15–17).

42. "Beware lest anyone cheat you through philosophy and empty deceit, according to the tradition of men, according to the basic principles of the world, and not according to Christ. For in Him dwells all the fullness of the Godhead bodily; and you are complete in Him, who is the head of all principality and power" (Col. 2:8–10).

43. "Having disarmed principalities and powers, He made a public spectacle of them, triumphing over them in it" (Col. 2:15).

Who shall separate us from the love of Christ? Shall tribulation, or distress, or persecution, or famine, or nakedness, or peril, or sword? As it is written: "For Your sake we are killed all day long; we are accounted as sheep for the slaughter." Yet in all these things we are more than conquerors through Him who loved us. For I am persuaded that neither death nor life, nor angels nor principalities nor powers, nor things present nor things to come, nor height nor depth, nor any other created thing, shall be able to separate us from the love of God which is in Christ Jesus our Lord.

—ROMANS 8:35–39

All hail the power of Jesus' name,
Let angles prostrate fall,
Bring forth the royal diadem
And crown Him Lord of all!
Hallelujah!

End Notes

Chapter 4

1 *Jonathan Edwards on the Great Awakening,* The National Humanities Institute, 1998.

2 *First Hand Great Awakening Testimonies in America,* Thomas Prince, Jr., 1743.

3 *The Biography of Elder David Purviance, A Sketch of the Great Kentucky Revival,* Levi Purviance, 1848, pp. 242–52.

4 *Autobiography of Peter Cartwright, the Backwoods Preacher,* edited by W. P. Strickland, New York: Carlton and Porter, 1856, pp. 30–33.

Chapter 6

1 *Revival! A People Saturated With God,* Brian Edwards, Evangelical Press, Duncan Campbell cassette tapes.

2 *History of Independence, Volume 3,* John Fletcher, page 69.

3 "Power From On High," John Greenfield, *Moravian C,* June 1989.

4 *Faithful Witness: The Life and Mission of William Carey,* Timothy George, Christian History Institute.

5 *A People Called Cumberland Presbyterians: A History Of The Cumberland Presbyterians,* Ben Barrus, Milton Baughn and Thomas Campbell, Publisher Wipf & Stock, February 1998.

6 Ibid.

7 Ibid.

8 Ibid.

9 Ibid.

10 Ibid.

11 Ibid.

12 *The Kehukee Association, The History of the Kehukee Association,* Lemuel Barkitt and Jesse Read, McArthur Baptist Library, Statesboro, Georgia.

13 *The D.L. Moody Collection: The Highlights of His Writings, Sermons, Anecdotes, and Life Story,* James S. Bell and Dwight Lyman Moody, Moody Press, January 1998.

14 *World Christian Encyclopedia,* Oxford University Press, 1982.

Chapter 7

1 *David Barrett's Lastest World Religions Statistics,* www.across.co.nz/World Religions Statistics.htm.

2 *World Christian Encyclopedia, A Comparative Survey of Churches and Religions in the Modern World,* David B. Barrett, George T. Kurian and Todd M. Johnson, Oxford University Press, 2001, pp. 1–23.

3 Ibid.

4 "Excerpts from The Writing of John Wesley and Other Family Members," Betty Jarboe, Scarecrow Printing, Inc., September 1990.

5 *The Ante-Nicene Fathers,* AGES Digital Library CD-ROM, Heritage Edition; Christian Library Volume 1; *Apostolic Fathers w/Justin Martyr and Irenaeus. Volume 2; Fathers of The Second Century Volume 3,* Latin Christianity, Tertullian, 1998.

6 *The Ante-Nicene Fathers,* AGES Digital Library CD-ROM, Heritage Edition; Christian Library Volume 1, *Apostolic Fathers w/Justin Martyr and Irenaeus; Volume 2 Fathers of The Second Century Volume 3,* Latin Christianity, Tertullian, 1998.

7 F.F. Bruce, *The New Testament Documents: Are They Reliable?,* Eerdmans Publishing, 1974, p. 16.

8 Ibid. pp. 1–20.

Chapter 8

1 *Hebrew Lexicon.*

Chapter 9

1 *Turn around Churches,* George Barna, Gospel Light Publications, February 1997.

Chapter 10

1 *The Road Less Traveled*, M. Scott Peck, Simon & Schuster Publishers.

2 *The Ante-Nicene Fathers*, AGES Digital Library CD-ROM, Heritage Edition; Christian Library Volume 3.

3 *The Ante-Nicene Fathers*, AGES Digital Library CD-ROM, Heritage Edition; Christian Library Volume 1.

Bibliography/Recommended Reading

1. *Christian England*, David L. Edwards, Eerdmans, Volume 1, 1980; Volume 2, 1983; Volume 3, 1984.
2. *World Christian Encyclopedia*, Oxford University Press, 1982.
3. *The Reformation*, Stephen P. Thompson, Green Haven Press, 1999.
4. *The Ante-Nicene Fathers*, AGES Digital Library CD-ROM, Heritage Edition; *Christian Library*, Volume 1; *Apostolic Fathers w/Justin Martyr and Irenaeus*, Volume 2; *Fathers of the Second Century*, Volume 3; *Latin Christianity*, Tertullian, 1998.
5. *Excellence of Christ*, Jonathan Edwards, AGES Digital Library CD-ROM, Heritage Edition; *Christian Library*, 1998.
6. *Revival Fire: Power From on High*, Charles Finney, AGES Digital Library CD-ROM, Heritage Edition; *Christian Library*, 1998.
7. *A Fresh Anointing*, Dr.R.T. Kendall, Thomas Nelson/Word, 1999.
8. *When God Shows Up: Staying Ready for the Unexpected*, Dr. R.T. Kendall, Gospel Light, 1998.
9. *Prevailing Prayer*, D.L. Moody, AGES Digital Library CD-ROM, Heritage Edition; *Christian Library*, 1998.
10. John Owen, *Justification by Faith*, AGES Digital Library CD-ROM, Heritage Edition; *Christian Library*, 1998.
11. *John Wesley, The Works of; John Wesley, The Biography of*, AGES Digital Library CD-ROM, Heritage Edition; *Christian Library*, 1998.
12. *A Life of John Calvin*, Alister E. McGrath, Basil Blackwell Publishers, 1990.
13. *Jesus the Healer*, E.W. Kenyon, Kenyon Gospel Publishing Society, 1968.

14. *Operation World,* Patrick Johnstone, Zondervan Publishing House, 1993.

15. *Powerlines: What Great Evangelicals Believed About the Holy Spirit,* Leona Frances Choy, Christian Publications, 1990.

16. *The Unshakable Kingdom and the Unchanging Person,* E. Stanley Jones, McNett Press, 1995.

17. *The Divine Conspiracy,* Dallas Willard, Harper SanFranscico, 1998.

18. *The Gospel of the Kingdom,* George Eldon Ladd., Eerdsman, 1999.

19. *In Defense of Miracles,* Edited by R.Douglas Givett and Gary R. Habermas, InterVarsity Press, 1997.

20. *The Great Evangelical Disaster,* Francis A. Schaeffer, Crossway Books, 1984.

21. *The Word of God With Power,* Jack Taylor, Broadman-Holman, 1993.

22. *After the Spirit Comes,* Jack Taylor, Broadman-Holman, 1983.

23. *Campbell Morgan Bible Teacher,* Harold Murray, Ambassador, 1958.

24. *Joy Unspeakable: Power & Renewal in the Holy Spirit,* Martyn Lloyd-Jones, Bethan Lloyd-Jones, Harold Shaw Publishers, 1984.

25. *Dictionary of Pentecostal and Charismatic Movements,* Edited by Stanley M. Burgess and Gary B. McGee, Zondervan Publishing House, 1988.

26. *Foundation Series: Foundation for Faith,* Volume 1; *Foundation Series: Repent and Believe,* Volume 2; Derek Prince, Sovereign World, 1986.

27. *Atonement: Your Appointment With God,* Derek Prince, Chosen Books, 2000.

28. *Spiritual Warfare,* Derek Prince, Whitaker House, 1987.

29. *The Holy Spirit in You*, Derek Prince, Whitaker House, 1987.

30. *Exercising Spiritual Gifts, Part I:* "Receive The Holy Spirit," Derek Prince, Video.

31. *Exercising Spiritual Gifts, Part II:* "Interpreting and Prophesying," Derek Prince, Video.

32. *Basics of Deliverance, Part 1:* "How to Identify The Enemy," Derek Prince, Video.

33. *The Power of Proclamation*, Derek Prince, Video.

34. *Purposes of Pentecost*, Derek Prince, Derek Prince Publications.

35. *Surprised by the Power of the Spirit*, Jack Deere, Zondervan Publishing House, 1993.

36. *Surprised by the Voice of God*, Jack Deere, Zondervan Publishing House, 1996.

37. *Christian Disciplines*, Oswald Chambers, Discovering House Publishers, 1936.

38. *The Elijah Task*, John and Paul Sanford, Logos International, 1977.

39. *Dominion Over Demons*, H.A. Maxwell Whyte, Banner Publishing, 1973.

40. How to Pray, R.A. Torrey, Fleming H. Revel, 1976.

41. *Destined for the Throne*, Paul E. Billheimer, Christian Literature Crusade, 1975.

42. *Concerning Spiritual Gifts*, Donald Gee, Gospel Publishing House, 1972.

43. *Jesus–God's Way of Healing and Power to Promote Health:* Miracle Ministry Of John G. Lake, Wilford H. Reidt, Harrison House, 1981.

44. *Handbook for Healing*, Charles and Frances Hunter, Hunter Books, 1987.

45. *God Tells the Man Who Cares*, A.W. Tozer, Christian Publications Inc., 1970.

46. *Mere Christianity*, C.W. Lewis, Macmillan Publishing Company, 1978.

47. *Faith That Prevails*, Smith Wigglesworth, Radiant Books, 1995.

48. *The Latent Power of the Soul*, Watchman Nee, Christian Fellowship Publishers, Inc., 1972.

49. *New Creation Realities*, E.W. Kenyon, Kenyon's Gospel Publishing Society, 1964.

50. *How to Conduct Spiritual Warfare*, Mary Garrison, 1980.

51. *Winning the Invisible War*, E.M. Bounds, Whitaker House, 1984.

52. *Discover Your God-Given Gifts*, Don and Katie Fortune, Chosen Books, 1987.

53. *Foxe's Book of Martyrs*, John Foxe, AGES Digital Library CD-ROM, Heritage Edition; Christian Library, 1998.

54. *The Second Coming of the Church*, George Barna, Word Publications, 1998.

About the Author

Charles Carrin's fifty-year ministry spans the final half of the twentieth century. In his youth he traveled with men who preached in the 1800s. For the first twenty-seven years of his ministry, Charles was a hyper-Calvinist Baptist pastor and Presbyterian seminarian who denied the miraculous works of the Holy Spirit. Midway in his ministry, that abruptly changed when he was forced to acknowledge scriptures he had previously ignored. It was a time of intense pain and testing.

Of the truths that emerged, Charles said:

> The facts were there. I saw them; but they were frightening. Terrifying. Worst of all, they had power to destroy my denominational ministry. Emotionally, I was not prepared to deal with that possibility; and at that point I had no hope that another, more wonderful ministry awaited me.

Charles emerged with an amazing empowering of the Holy Spirit. Today, his ministry centers on the visible demonstration of the Spirit and imparting of His gifts. As an evangelist/writer, Charles' articles have appeared in major Christian magazines in the United States and abroad. He travels extensively, teaching believers how to operate in the power of the Spirit.

Charles Carrin Ministries
P.O. Drawer 800, Boynton Beach, FL 33425-0800
Fax: (561) 364-4119

Visit the following website:
www.CharlesCarrinMinistries.com

Other books by Charles Carrin:
Sunrise of David / Sunrise of Saul
On Whose Authority?
The Battering Ram of God